# FINANCE IN YOUR OWN BUSINESS

Series editor: Eric Parker
Kurt Illetschko
Lesley-Caren Johnson

ISBN: 978-1-920434-13-7

First edition, first impression 2011

Published jointly by
Bookstorm (Pty) Limited and Pan Macmillan South Africa
PO Box 4532                          Private Bag X19
Northcliff, 2115                     Northlands, 2116
Johannesburg                         Johannesburg
South Africa                         South Africa
www.bookstorm.co.za                  www.panmacmillan.co.za

Distributed by Pan Macmillan
Via Booksite Afrika

Edited by Reneé Ferreira and Jeannie van den Heever
Proofread by Salome Smit
Cover design by René de Wet
Typeset by Lebone Publishing Services, Cape Town
Printed and bound buy Ultra Litho (Pty) Limited

# CONTENTS

**Foreword** ...................................................................  v

### 1. HOW TO RAISE FINANCE FOR YOUR BUSINESS

Introduction .....................................................  1

Formulate your plans .....................................  4

Types of finance ............................................  12

Sources of finance .........................................  15

Getting it down on paper ...............................  35

Package and sell your project! ......................  46

Conclusion .....................................................  53

### 2. FINANCE FOR NON-FINANCIAL PEOPLE

Introduction .....................................................  57

Financial and management accounts ...............  58

The income statement ...................................  64

The balance sheet ..........................................  79

Interpreting the financial information ...........  87

Cash flow management ..................................  92

Budgeting and business planning ..................  106

## 3. FIFTEEN KEY BUSINESS CALCULATIONS

Introduction ........................................................ 117

The importance of performing periodic
business calculations ......................................... 118

Reasons why businesses fail .............................. 119

Which financial statements will you need? ....... 124

The fifteen critical business calculations ........... 128

## APPENDICES

Appendix 1: Extract from the Companies
Act ..................................................................... 168

Appendix 2: Financial reporting requirements
and the Public Interest Score ............................ 170

Appendix 3: Tax relief for small businesses .... 172

Appendix 4: Table of financial benchmarks
per industry ........................................................ 175

Appendix 5: Glossary of financial terms ........... 179

Appendix 6: Calculations overview ................... 183

**INDEX** ....................................................... **190**

# FOREWORD

We live in a period of uncertainty and change. Unemployment is rampant, and those who think that their jobs are secure need to face up to the reality that the proverbial 'job for life' is rapidly becoming as extinct as the dodo.

Readers of this book will have realised that the world is full of opportunities, with entrepreneurship topping all others. As an entrepreneur, you have taken charge of your destiny and are ready to show what you are really capable of – and in the process you plan to build substantial wealth that you and your family can enjoy.

This book is designed to give you, the business owner, the essential advice you need to succeed in your entrepreneurial venture. The book is short and to the point, providing practical information on how to run your business effectively.

Let me close by saying that becoming an entrepreneur is like setting out on an exciting journey. The path may be perilous at times, but once you arrive at your destination you will feel more satisfaction than you ever dared to expect. From one entrepreneur to another – you have my word on that!

*Eric*

**Eric Parker**
**Franchising Plus**

# HOW TO RAISE FINANCE FOR YOUR BUSINESS

*Kurt Illetschko*

## INTRODUCTION

There is general consensus that small business holds the key to the continued growth of the South African economy, and with good reason. Large companies used to be major creators of employment opportunities in the past but this is no longer the case. Pressure resulting from the free flow of goods and services across global markets forced them to become more competitive. This resulted in mergers, increased mechanisation and job losses. Make no mistake – this trend is here to stay!

For better or worse, small businesses cannot afford the luxury of mechanising everything. It follows that if more small businesses are established or expanded, more jobs will be created. Government has recognised this and offers support. Several programmes have been put in place, but there are few takers!

It almost seems as if people are reluctant to either become entrepreneurs or expand their existing businesses. Perhaps this is caused by a shortage of role models. Until recently, education systems focused squarely on the creation of future employees for big corporations and government departments.

*More and more employees are retrenched
from large companies*

Entrepreneurship as a career option was not given the prominence it deserves.

Research carried out by the Global Entrepreneurship Monitor (GEM) highlights this sad state of affairs. The GEM is a major international research study aimed at increasing the understanding of entrepreneurship. To ensure that apples are compared with apples, the organisation has developed a *Total Entrepreneurial Activity index*. This index measures the proportion of a country's adults who are involved in starting or running a new business.

There is no shortage of interest. Thousands of individuals regularly attend small business seminars, visit small business websites and purchase books on entrepreneurship. Ask them what stops them from actually starting a business and they will tell you that it is lack of access to funding. In many instances, this is a poor excuse for failure to act.

All available evidence suggests that funding for small businesses is available. What is in short supply are entrepreneurs who can demonstrate to lenders that their money will be safe. This needs to be addressed.

In addition to proving their technical expertise, entrepreneurs need to demonstrate their ability to manage money responsibly. Unfortunately, individuals who have the ability to do this appear to be as rare as hen's teeth. Should this sound like a harsh generalisation to you, ask any banker. He or she will confirm that most of the people who approach the bank for loans are barely able to quantify *how much* money they need. When asked *what type* of finance they think would be the most appropriate, they are out of their depth.

## The objective of this chapter

Working through this chapter will help you realise that raising finance for your business is a process, not an event. And this process is an ongoing one. Securing start-up finance only means that you have cleared the first hurdle. As your business expands, it is likely to need additional funding. Simply walking into your banker's office and asking him or her for money is unlikely to succeed. Once you have worked through this chapter, you will know that a fundamentally different approach is required.

However, knowledge is useless unless it is followed by meaningful action. This chapter will guide you every step of the way. You will learn how to prepare a realistic funding request and present it with the passion needed to convince a potentially sceptical funder. And you will also know how to manage investor relations, another essential tool in the quest for funding that is frequently neglected.

## Who will benefit from reading this chapter?

Newcomers to the business scene will learn how to secure start-up finance. Established entrepreneurs needing finance for expansion will benefit as well. Money is available – the trick is to gain access. If this is your problem, this chapter offers proven ways of solving it.

## FORMULATE YOUR PLANS

Before you approach anyone for finance, you need to know what you want to do and how you intend to turn your plans into reality. Some people are quick to say that their only rationale for going into business is the desire to make lots of money as quickly as possible. This could be problematic!

Building a successful business rarely happens overnight, and a lot of hard work is involved. Research has shown that the expectation of making lots of money tends to lose its allure long before the new business delivers meaningful profits. To stay the course, you need to have passion for what you want to do.

As the owner of a small business, you *are* the business. If you are less than enthusiastic about it, how can you expect others to react differently? By 'others' we mean staff, customers, suppliers and any other stakeholders. They will soon sense your lack of enthusiasm and be put off by it. To build a successful business in this climate is extremely difficult. We suggest that you proceed as follows.

## Develop the concept

Begin by identifying what you are good at and love doing. Make a list of these activities. Next, examine them one

*Don't go into business just to make money –*
*you must have a passion for what you do*

by one for their commercial viability. Lastly, consider the likelihood of a business built around this activity being sustainable. The following checklist will guide you.

## How to develop a viable concept

### Personal considerations

- What do I really like doing?
- Realistically speaking, am I good at doing it?
- Will I enjoy doing it professionally for the next five to seven years?
- Can I deal with all the other tasks involved in managing a business?
- Will my health stand up to the demands of establishing a business?
- How does my family feel about me going into business – will they be supportive?
- Can I live with the idea of '24/7 working weeks' and little social life?

### The market

- Is it possible to build a viable business around the product?
- Does a well-established market for the product exist?
- Who are my prospective customers?
- Is the market of sufficient size to accommodate an additional supplier?
- Who are the main competitors in this sector?
- What are their respective strengths and weaknesses?
- Are they involved in an ongoing price war?
- How will I compete against them without eroding the profitability of my business?

### Financial aspects

- Will I be able to raise sufficient capital?
- How will I finance living expenses until the business can afford to pay me a salary?
- Do I have a history of handling money responsibly?
- How will it affect me, and my family, if the business fails?

## Consider the implementation phase

To begin with, you should give some thought to the infrastructure you need to create. At this stage, broad brushstrokes will suffice. We will show you how to refine it at a later stage.

*Draw up a wish list of all the items you think you need*

## Physical infrastructure

Draw up a wish list of all the items you think you will need.

### *Premises*

Describe the ideal premises, their preferred location and any special features they should have. Examples would be exposure to passing trade, ample customer parking, access to heavy-duty power supply and other utilities, etc.

### *Equipment and supplies*

- In the case of a retail business, you would list signage, furniture, furnishings, décor and store equipment.

- If you plan to start a manufacturing business, you will need to compile a list of processing and handling equipment.

- No matter what type of business you plan to start, you need to make provision for its administration. This may entail computers and point-of-sale equipment, desks and chairs, filing cabinets, stationery and consumables.

## Sources of supply

Whatever business sector you are in, chances are that you will depend on a regular supply of raw materials or finished goods. You should investigate this aspect carefully.

- Are the products you need always available, or do shortages occur? If so, what alternatives are there?

- Does one supplier dominate the market? If so, you could be vulnerable. Let us assume, for example, that a powerful supplier to the sector acquires one of your competitors and wants to keep you out of the market. You could be forced to pay excessive prices for your supplies, or be cut off altogether. (You could address the Competition Board for redress, but who wants to invest time and energy in this unless it is absolutely unavoidable?)

> It is best to establish good relations with potential suppliers at an early stage. In some instances, it may even be advisable to enter into a long-term supply contract. Should you decide to do that, be careful not to over-commit yourself.

### Staff considerations

Unless the business you plan to establish is extremely small to begin with and you expect it to stay this way for some time, you will need to hire staff. You need to satisfy yourself that an adequate pool of trained workers is available. A skills shortage could inflate salaries. It would also make it difficult to retain people and forge them into a dependable team.

### Administration of the business

Earlier in this chapter, we stated the need to make provision for computers, etc. However, there is more to the effective administration of a business than equipment and furniture. Potential funders want to be convinced that you understand the impact of effective administration on the chances of your business succeeding.

Among other things, they will expect you to keep track of the financial performance of your business. To do this effectively, you need to be comfortable reading and interpreting management accounts and financial reports. Should your expertise in this field be weak, now is the time to make amends.

- Read Chapters 2 and 3 of this book, which cover issues regarding financial management.

- Several reputable colleges offer short courses on business accounting. Attending one will be well worth your while, both in terms of time and money.

> Failure to keep your business's books of account up to date can be compared to playing cricket without someone keeping score. Before long, nobody will know what is really going on. This can only result in chaos!

### The need for flexibility

Throughout this section, we have provided examples of possible problems. Some of them may not affect you. That is OK; we just want to get you thinking. As you plan the establishment of your business, you may uncover problem areas you did not anticipate. In some instances, just being aware of them may enable you to avoid them. In other instances, avoiding them may not be possible, but at least you are aware of their existence before you commit yourself to any particular course of action.

In the case of a retail business, for example, you may find it difficult to secure your dream site at a rental the business can afford. Shopping centres are notoriously inflexible and your chances of negotiating a significant decrease in rental are low. You may be tempted to sign up at the higher rental and hope for the best. Or you may settle for a less-than-

*Stay flexible*

perfect site. Both approaches could reduce your business's chances of success.

If faced with such a dilemma, it is best to revisit your assumptions and find the most acceptable solution.

- Are you confident that the ideal site will help you to increase sales significantly? Redo your financial projections. Should the revised level of sales allow you to pay the higher rental and still make a profit, go for it! Risk taking is OK as long as it is a calculated risk!

- Should you be unable to justify paying the higher rent, an alternative approach is needed. How about modifying your product range? You can do that either by adding value or by presenting it differently. The objective would be to change your target market so that you can either increase the mark-up percentage or make your business less site-dependent.

By reducing dependency on passing trade, you could turn your business into a 'destination store'. Destination store means that your business does not depend on passing trade. Rather, your customers would actually want to visit your store. It also means that rentals will be significantly cheaper.

The following examples illustrate this point:

- A fast-food restaurant depends for its business largely on passing trade. Unless the right site can be found, the business will never reach its full potential. Put your plans on hold until the right site becomes available.

- The typical five-star restaurant is far less site-dependent. If you manage to create the right kind of buzz, people will want to visit. Within reason, the geographic location will become a secondary consideration.

# TYPES OF FINANCE

Business finance falls into two major groupings, namely equity finance and loan finance. In practice, no business can exist on loan finance alone. If loan funding is the sole source of finance, the resulting repayments will be so high that it could derail the business. For this reason, we will deal with equity finance first.

## Equity finance

Equity finance is money the owners of an unregistered business or the shareholders of a company invest in the business. For the purposes of this section, we will refer to them collectively as shareholders from now on.

Equity finance is an investment in the business – once made, the business 'owns' it. To unlock this investment, a shareholder would have to sell his or her share of the business to another investor. If shareholders want their money back but no purchaser can be found, the business has to be liquidated.

Shareholders have no guarantee that they will receive their money back. Nor does the money they invest bear interest. Instead, shareholders acquire ownership of the business and participate in its profits and losses. If the business has more than one shareholder, a pro rata allocation of shares based on the invested amount is customary. This is, however, a matter for negotiation.

As a business becomes established, it builds up its customer base and its brand becomes better known. This creates additional value, known as *goodwill*. In addition to being entitled to a share of profits, shareholders also share in the goodwill value of the business. This means that if the business does well, a shareholder who sells his or her shares can look forward to a substantial windfall.

### Summary of salient points

- In accounting terms, equity is neither a loan nor a liability. It is reflected in the business's accounting records as shareholders' equity. This has the effect of strengthening the business's balance sheet. The higher the amount of shareholders' equity, the more solid the business is perceived to be.

- Investors are entitled to a share of the profits the business generates. If no profit is made, shareholders are not entitled to receive anything.

- Should you decide at some future date to buy out other shareholders, they will expect to be paid back their investment. In addition, they are entitled to a share of the value of the business at that time, made up of assets and goodwill.

- Ordinarily, shareholders cannot secure their investment. Should the business fail, claims by preferred creditors have to be satisfied before shareholders' interests will be considered. This means that, in practice, should the business fail, shareholders have little hope of getting their money back. Their investment could be lost and they would not have a claim against other shareholders.

*Equity finance is money the owners invest in the business*

*Loan finance is borrowed money*

## Loan finance

Loan finance is money that is borrowed on behalf of the business. It could be repayable as a lump sum. More commonly, loans are repaid in a series of instalments, usually monthly by a specific date.

When negotiating loan finance for a new business, you should request a repayment holiday. This means that for an agreed period, say the first three to four months, you make interest payments only. Most commercial banks know that the cash flow of a new business will be weak and will therefore agree to this request.

### *Summary of salient points*

- This type of transaction is a purely financial one and business performance has no bearing on it. Whether the business makes a profit or not is of no direct concern to the lender. In accounting terms, loan finance is shown in the business's accounting records as a *liability*. This has the effect of weakening the business's balance sheet.

- Loan instalments and interest are payable as set out in the loan agreement.

- The lender is not entitled to a share of profits.

- Shareholders can grant loans to the business. Such loans are shown in the *shareholders' loan accounts*. To protect themselves, external lenders and creditors are likely to insist that shareholders' loan accounts are subordinated in their favour. In practical terms, this means that, should the business experience financial problems, shareholders are unlikely to receive a payout.

In the small business environment, banks remain the main source of loan capital. However, banks' expectations continue to be quite rigid. To qualify for bank finance on acceptable terms, you need to consider alternative forms of finance first.

# SOURCES OF FINANCE

In the small business environment, loans are typically the main source of finance and banks the main providers. Unless the business has some equity, however, loan finance will be difficult to obtain. In this section, we introduce you to the different sources of finance and explain their respective characteristics.

## Equity finance
### Own funds

Unless you are able to inject some money of your own into the business, your best efforts to attract funding may be doomed. Your own contribution could come from savings, or you could raise cash by disposing of personal assets you can do without at this stage.

Should circumstances demand that you reduce your standard of living for a while, you should be willing to do that. Should you own a holiday home, a second car or any other trappings of modern-day living, consider selling them off. In the near future, you are unlikely to enjoy them anyway.

Explain to your family that this is a temporary measure. As soon as your start-up venture has developed into a substantial business, you will be able to make up for it, and more.

You should think twice, however, before you sell off your home to raise cash, for the following reasons:

- Your equity may be low. If so, once you have paid off the mortgage/bond, little cash will be left over.

- Once sold, your home can no longer serve as surety for a bank loan.

- You would have to find alternative accommodation. This could be expensive.

If you own a luxury home and consider it prudent to scale down for a while, consider renting it out and moving to less lavish accommodation. This way, you retain an income-producing asset that remains available as surety.

### Shareholders working in the business

Perhaps you know someone you are convinced you could work with effectively. If so, you could consider inviting this person to join you in your venture. You could offer him or her part-ownership of the business in exchange for working in the business and making a financial contribution. This has potential advantages and disadvantages, and we advise you to weigh them up with care.

### Advantages

- *Enhanced capital base:* Additional shareholders' cash injections increase the business's capital base.

- *Shared responsibilities:* Having fellow shareholders allows you to spread the burden. In addition to splitting the investment and business risk, you could share management responsibility. For example, one of you could go on leave while the other continues to take care of business.

- *Complementary strengths:* Ideally, the respective strengths and weaknesses of your fellow shareholders should complement one another. In a manufacturing business, for example, a person with a strong technical bias, a marketing-oriented individual and an administrator could make a formidable team. It would be even better if one of you has a basic understanding of labour legislation as well.

- *Strong commitment:* It is safe to assume that your fellow shareholders will be as committed to the business as you are. While an employee may decide to leave should the going get tough, a shareholder is far less likely to choose this option.

### Disadvantages

- *Dilution of ownership:* Having fellow shareholders means that decisions must be made by consensus. This could limit your ability to move forward.

- *Financial implications:* It is customary for shareholders who work in the business to draw a salary. This is set by arrangement, usually in relation to the value each individual adds. This is rarely an issue because you would have had to pay someone anyway. However, shareholders are also entitled to a share of the business's profits. This is one area of potential conflict. You may want to reinvest but your fellow shareholders may want to draw the money out.

Unless you and your fellow shareholders have a similar vision for the business and get on really well, such an arrangement could develop into a nightmare, so be careful whom you choose. Moreover, you should always insist on a written agreement, drafted by an attorney with proven expertise in this field.

### Shareholders represented on the board

Should you find shareholders who do not plan to work in the business, personal compatibility may be less of an issue. What you need to watch out for, however, are their expectations. Although they do not work in the business, these shareholders will have a say in the way the business is operated. And unless they are members of your family or close friends who want to help you, they may have unrealistic expectations.

Depending on the percentage of their shareholding, they could, for example, dictate a dividend policy that does not allow the business to grow. Or they could decide to sell out at a time when you do not have the liquidity to repurchase the shares.

A shareholders' agreement, drafted by a competent attorney, will safeguard the interests of all parties. At the same time, it will protect you from unwanted surprises.

### Sleeping partners

On occasion, individuals who neither want to work in the business nor become involved in its management inject funds. This has the potential of a match made in heaven, but only if it stays this way.

*Sleeping partner*

Few things can be worse than ending up with someone who joins the business as a 'sleeping partner' and then changes his or her tune. Not long after you have invested the money he or she has advanced you, the sleeping partner experiences a change of heart and starts second-guessing every decision you make.

Should you have to buy out such an individual, it could play havoc with your cash flow. Trying to accommodate his or her whims could prevent you from making sound management decisions. Once again, a properly drafted agreement is your only protection.

Starting or expanding a small business should never revolve around legal agreements. There are instances, however, when this is unavoidable. Taking on business partners is definitely one of them. When it comes to the drafting of agreements involving the allocation of shares and other investment issues, a do-it-yourself approach is not recommended. As the Americans say: *'The guy who acts as his own attorney has a fool for a client!'*

### Venture capital funding

Venture capitalists take equity stakes in businesses that display certain characteristics. What they are primarily looking for is strong growth potential. They tend to be far less risk-averse than bankers. And in addition to making an equity invest-ment, venture capitalists take an active hand in the business's management. Their objective is to grow the business to a level where it can be sold at a significant capital profit. The ultimate dream of any venture capitalist is to prepare a business for a successful listing on the stock exchange.

The typical venture capitalist will have an investment horizon of between five and seven years. He or she will formulate an exit strategy at the outset. This means that, at the end of this period, venture capitalists want to sell their stake in the business at a huge capital profit. Should you want to grow your business slowly and in a controlled fashion, a venture capitalist may not be the right kind of business partner for you.

During the period of their involvement, venture capitalists will take an active hand in steering the business and driving its growth. Some will make their expertise available without drawing a salary. They may even forego dividend payouts so that profits can be reinvested. However, at the end of the period, they will expect a windfall equalling at least 30% compound return on their original investment.

In reality, very few small businesses show sufficient growth potential at the start-up stage to attract a venture capitalist's interest. Venture capitalists will usually look for a trading history of at least three years. The business should also display above-average potential for growth. However, exceptions do exist, so it is worthwhile exploring this option.

### Retained earnings

You should plan from the outset to reinvest part of the profits your business generates. If you do this methodically and limit personal spending until the business can really afford it, two things will happen:

1. You create an attractive form of finance because it is cheap and you do not have to pay it back.

2. Your funders will be impressed with your display of spending discipline and more agreeable to providing additional funding for expansion.

## Raising bank finance

Banks continue to be the main source of loan finance for small businesses. They generally offer loan finance rather than equity finance, but theirs is not a one-size-fits-all approach. Banks offer a wide range of products, but you need to know what to ask for.

### *Overdraft*

This is the most common form of bank loan, and the easiest to obtain. Once an overdraft limit has been autho-rised, you are able to draw on your bank account up to the agreed limit, just as if you had the money in the bank. Your bank is likely to charge you a facility fee for making the overdraft available. It will also charge you interest on the daily debit balance.

An overdraft should be seen as bridging finance. The bank's expectation is that your account balance should fluctuate. It should show a credit balance at least some of the time. (This means that, on occasion, the business's account should show a positive balance.)

### *Advantage*

What makes overdraft finance so attractive is the fact that interest is calculated on a daily basis. If you do not use it, you do not pay interest.

*The bank can withdraw your overdraft at any time,
thus cutting off your lifeline*

### Disadvantage

The problem with overdraft finance is that your banker has the right to call it up at short notice. Should this happen, it may not be a reflection of the way you conduct your business. Some economist at the bank's head office may get the idea that your industry sector has become a bit risky. Or your bank wishes to reduce its exposure in the small business sector. If, as a result of such policy decisions, your local bank manager receives an instruction to withdraw your overdraft, he or she would have no option but to do so. For this reason alone, an overdraft should never be used to finance investments of a long-term nature.

### Factoring

If you trade in the business-to-business sector, you will be forced to extend credit to your customers. This will tie up working capital and could limit your ability to grow the business. You can keep your debtors book low by offering customers incentives for early settlement. This will reduce the amount of money outstanding but it will not eliminate it altogether.

One way around this problem is to turn your debtors book into cash by 'selling' it to a finance house; this is known as 'factoring'. It is an expensive form of finance, and the finance house may impose certain conditions. It will, for example, want to vet your customers' credit ratings, and it will set minimum transaction values.

Once an agreement has been signed, the finance house will advance you a portion of outstanding invoice values, probably around 80%. As soon as your customers pay the finance house, you receive the balance, less its fees. However, you continue to carry the full credit risk. Should one of your customers fail to pay, the finance house will recoup the advance plus its fee from you.

### Credit card finance

Credit card finance is short-term finance. It is attractive because if you plan your spending correctly, you can get up to 55 days finance interest-free. Budget facilities, where you can pay off the balance over three, six or 12 months, are also available, but pre-set credit limits tend to reduce the usefulness of this option. Once you exceed the free finance period, credit card finance becomes expensive. As a rule, it should only be used to fund short-term working capital needs.

### Term loan finance

The previous financing options have one thing in common: They provide short-term finance. To raise funds for longer periods, you need to take out a term loan. Term loans are usually offered for periods of between 36 and 60 months. They are repayable in monthly instalments to which interest will be added.

> To set the ball rolling, you need to present your banker with a loan proposal, backed by a viable business plan. The loan proposal needs to set out what you need the money for, for how long you need it, when you propose to repay it and what surety you can offer.

On approval of your application, the bank will enter into a written loan agreement with you that will contain the agreed terms and conditions. Loan capital can be used to finance the purchase of equipment, furniture and initial stock, or even as working capital.

#### *Advantages*

- Term loans are granted for a fixed period. Ordinarily, such a loan cannot be recalled before the agreed time. This enables you to make long-term investment decisions.

- Interest rates charged for term loans are generally lower than those charged for overdraft finance. (Given fluctuations in the market, the interest rate is unlikely to be fixed in advance. What will be fixed is the percentage point differential to the ruling prime rate.)

#### *Disadvantages*

- A term loan is granted for a fixed period. You will pay interest on the outstanding balance even if your current account with the same bank is in credit.

- The bank's undertaking not to recall the loan prematurely is not absolute. If you fall into arrears with agreed repayments, the bank can ask for the complete outstanding balance.

## Asset finance

Although term loans are usually the cheapest form of finance, they do need to be secured. Should this create problems, you could consider asset finance as an alternative. This means that the asset you purchase is used as part-security for the loan. See also the box on the following page.

The main options of asset finance are:

### Instalment sale

This is a credit agreement. You provide the bank with detailed information on the item you wish to purchase. The bank purchases the item from the supplier and sells it on to you. You pay the purchase price, plus interest, to the bank in agreed monthly instalments over a negotiated period. Ownership of the item remains with the bank until you have made the final payment. At that point, you become the owner of the item. (This form of financing was previously known as hire purchase finance.)

### Rental agreement

If you are in a high-tech business and need to replace equipment frequently, renting it could be your best option. Depending on the projected residual value of the equipment, repayments could be relatively low. (Residual value is the projected value of the item at the end of the rental period.)

You enjoy the uninterrupted use of the item for a predetermined period, but you never gain ownership. This type of arrangement is similar to renting a property. The finance house will consider such an arrangement only if it is reasonably certain that, at the end of the rental period, it can sell the item at its residual value.

### Financial lease agreement

The bank purchases the item and you enjoy its uninterrupted use. At the end of the agreed period, you have the option to purchase the item from the finance house, usually at its residual value. As lease charges are fully tax deductible, the use of this form of financing may, subject to individual circumstances, result in significant tax advantages.

> All forms of asset finance can be structured to the needs of the business. The usefulness and expected lifespan of the asset will be taken into account. Agreements for asset finance are offered for periods of between 12 and 60 months. In most instances, a deposit is payable. Moreover, the finance house or bank will protect its interest in the item by retaining ownership. It will also request you to sign a personal guarantee.

### Letter of guarantee

As you set up a new business, you will be asked to pay a myriad of deposits. For example, your landlord will demand a rent deposit. Suppliers of electricity, water and other utilities will expect the same, and so on. To conserve scarce cash reserves, you may want to offer letters of guarantee instead.

Subject to your credit rating, your bank will issue these letters – at a price. Because funds are committed and the bank accepts a risk, you will be charged a facilities fee. However, no money is actually paid out so this fee should be lower than the overdraft rate.

## Alternative sources of finance

### Soft loans

Soft loans are primarily intended to help you beef up the equity portion of your business's capital base. You can ask a family member or a friend to grant you a loan that is unsecured and open-ended. This means that the lender agrees to provide the loan without security and without a fixed repayment date. The repayment of bank loans and other secured obligations will take priority.

On the surface of it, soft loans may appear to be an attractive option for small business finance. This form of finance can have some drawbacks, however, and you need to be aware of them:

- Some people's characters change in strange ways after they have lent you money. They may feel that they are

*Be careful of soft loans: Some people's characters change after they have lent you money*

entitled to tell you how to operate the business, or even how to live your life. This can result in the breakdown of relationships.

- On occasion, grantors of soft loans have been known to behave like part-owners of the business. They may consider it their right to remove goods from the business, or utilise the business's services excessively without paying for them. This can have a disastrous effect on the gross profit ratio of a small business.

- The lender may encounter unexpected financial problems and demand repayment of the loan at a time when the business's cash flow makes it difficult to oblige.

- Should the business fail, losses encountered by loved ones could impact negatively on valuable personal relationships.

---

Anecdotal evidence suggests that many successful entrepreneurs have established their businesses with the help of families and friends. My advice would be that if you go this route, have an attorney draw up a formal loan agreement. This agreement should record the arrangement in detail. This protects the interests of both parties and prevents misunderstandings.

---

### Sweat equity

If you are determined to make a go of your planned venture but cannot raise the capital you need, 'sweat equity' may be an option. This means that you have to convince an individual to put up the funding you need. Your contribution to the venture would consist of the supply of expertise and labour. Should you consider this option, you should know in advance how it works.

### *Structuring a sweat equity deal*

The way such deals are structured is open to negotiation. Binding models do not exist but a typical scenario of this kind would unfold as follows:

- You will be employed in a business owned by the investor. Upon proving yourself, you will be offered the chance to take over the business or set up a branch operation.

- Unless the investor knows you well, he or she is likely to insist on a trial period. This is not a bad thing. It gives both parties a chance to get to know each another.

- Initially, you may have to be content with a moderate salary. You should, however, insist on becoming a part-owner of the business from the outset, even if the transfer of shares is delayed until you pay for them.

- Traditionally, it has been difficult to locate investors prepared to enter into such an arrangement.

### *Financing arrangements*

- You earn an agreed percentage of the new business's profits from the outset. The balance of the profits goes to the investor.

- Your profit share is paid into a trust account where it is allowed to accumulate. Once a predetermined sum becomes available, it will be used to pay for your share of the business.

You should insist that the value of the business is laid down upfront, based on its asset value at the time. Should the purchase price be based on the value of the business at the time of transfer, you will be penalised for working hard and creating value in the form of goodwill.

### Forming a syndicate

Should you be well known within your industry sector and enjoy the respect of your peers, you could form a syndicate. This means that you assemble a number of investors who back your venture. Each member of the syndicate contributes a relatively small amount. Added together, these contributions can make up a sizeable sum.

Keep in mind, though, that unlike family and friends, members of an investment syndicate have no interest in supporting your dream. They are in it for the money. Unless the arrangement is carefully managed, everyone will try to steer the business in a different direction. And should the venture hit a rough spot, investors may call for it to be closed down. This could destroy a business that is intrinsically viable. If properly structured, however, syndicates can work to the benefit of all stakeholders.

### Community financing

Communal savings accounts (*stokvels*) are a uniquely South African finance mechanism. They are community-based and collect funds from members. These funds are lent to one member at a time, for example to finance the building of a residential dwelling.

Many communal savings accounts exist in South Africa and their collective investment capacity is estimated to run into billions of rands per annum. As far as we could establish, they do not appear to feature as a significant source of capital for serious business start-ups at this stage. This does not mean, however, that the stokvel movement could not develop into something big in future.

In Asian countries, notably Indonesia, similar schemes are used extensively to fund business start-ups. Some of these companies have developed into spectacular success stories. They repaid their loans with interest and continue to provide support to the communities that created them.

### Micro lenders

Micro lenders are a possible source of capital but, to this day, their reputation as providers of business finance remains poor. They focus on lending rather than investing. They are also notorious for charging excessive rates of interest. Anecdotal evidence suggests that rogue elements among them apply somewhat unorthodox collection methods, leaving defaulters with lacerations and worse.

It is only fair to acknowledge that, more recently, this sector has made serious attempts to clean up its image.

*Communal savings accounts are community-based*

Such things take time, however, and it is probably best to take a wait-and-see attitude. Should you decide to deal with a micro lender, make sure that you understand the terms. It is best to deal with a company that subscribes to the sector's code of ethics.

### Mortgage/bond finance

If the amount you need to raise is relatively small, you should consider taking out a second mortgage/bond over your home. Mortgage/bond finance is significantly cheaper than traditional small business finance. Should the thought of putting your residential dwelling at risk make you uncomfortable, consider this: Every lender will insist on a personal guarantee from you. Taking out a second mortgage/bond does not increase your risk at all.

> Circumstances vary and no single form of finance is ideal for every purpose. Consider the needs of your business carefully before you decide on your preferred funding mix. Furthermore, it is important to take into account the effects of the National Credit Act and Consumer Protection Act on funding activities.

*Franchising could be seen as a financing mechanism*

## Franchising

Franchising is not a financing mechanism per se. However, franchising can impact on the way you structure the financial affairs of your business in various ways.

### Introduction

Franchising is an arrangement between the franchisor (the provider of the franchise) and the franchisee (the person who makes an investment in a franchise).

### *The franchisor*

The franchisor is the owner of a recognised brand. He or she has also developed a product and a tried-and-tested system for the successful operation of the business. The franchisor has now decided to expand the business into a regional, national or even international concern. To achieve this, the franchisor:

- allows carefully selected individuals access to the business's brand name, product range, systems and procedures

- provides franchisees with comprehensive initial training and ongoing training and support in all aspects of operating the business

- continues to control the trademark as well as the way in which the product is offered to the public

- receives an initial lump sum payment and ongoing fees from franchisees.

### *The franchisee*

The franchisee is an individual who wishes to own and operate a business but is reluctant to go it alone. By investing in a franchise, he or she acquires the rights to a proven business package, plus access to initial and ongoing training and support.

### Financial implications

The reason why we deal with franchising, albeit briefly, in a book on finance is twofold.

1. By franchising their businesses, franchisors are able to expand their businesses quicker than would otherwise be the case.

   - Franchisees pay an upfront fee in exchange for admission to the network. The franchisor can use these funds to establish an infrastructure and promote the brand.

   - Franchisees are responsible for set-up costs and working capital. This enables the franchisor to grow quicker than would otherwise be the case.

   Viewed from this angle, franchising could be seen as a finance mechanism for prospective franchisors, with one important proviso. In a business context, the word *franchise* is understood to mean *blueprint for business success*. It would be unethical to franchise a business at the start-up stage. To qualify as a franchise, the business should have a proven record of success stretching over at least two years. The impact of the Consumer Protection Act on franchise arrangements must also be taken into account.

2. Seen from a prospective franchisee's viewpoint, bankers know that franchisees enjoy a significantly better chance of success than independent start-ups. For this reason alone, they will receive a much warmer welcome. Moreover, various loan schemes dedicated to franchise finance are available.

# GETTING IT DOWN ON PAPER

To increase the odds of acceptance, any funding application needs to be supported by a well-thought-out business plan and a set of financial projections. Providing you with detailed guidelines on how to prepare these documents would exceed the parameters of this book. Several excellent publications dealing with this topic are available and the major banks offer a template for the completion of business plans.

The purpose of this section is to provide you with pointers on how to make your documentation stand out and make potential investors take notice.

## The funding proposal

Your funding proposal should state how much money you need, what you need it for, by when you need it and how you propose to repay it.

*Prepare properly when you apply for a bank loan*

### Applying for a bank loan

Unless the amount you wish to raise is extremely small, your contact at the bank is unlikely to make an immediate decision. He or she will pass the application on to the bank's loan committee, together with a recommendation.

The bank's loan committee meets at regular intervals to review loan applications and assess their merits. All major banks work this way and, for security reasons, the identities of the members of the loan committee are kept a carefully guarded secret. As the members of the loan committee will never meet you, they will base their decision on the written information you prepare for them.

The recommendation of the banker who interviewed you will be taken into account. However, the quality of the application and the results of the background check the bank will have commissioned are the decisive factors.

Each bank has its own set of documents it will expect you to complete but the basic information required is virtually identical. The banker who interviews you will give you a set of forms to complete, turning this into a case of 'filling in the blanks'. Preparing the necessary information beforehand will simplify this task, and the following checklist will guide you.

---

### Checklist: Information you should prepare in advance

To complete a bank's loan application, you should have the following information available:

#### Name and address details

Your full name(s), physical address, postal address, telephone number(s), cell phone number(s) and e-mail address.

---

### Residential property

Is the place where you live owned or rented? How long have you stayed at this address? (If you have stayed there for less than three years, your previous residential address will also be required.)

### Personal details

Age, nationality and residence status.

Marital status. If you are married or divorced, you will need a certified copy of the relevant contract or decree. If applicable, you need to provide personal details of your spouse and children.

### Educational background

Highest standard passed and year, details of degrees/diplomas/ certificates earned and institutions, details of formal apprenticeship training completed and details of formal business skills training/ experience.

### Employment history

Depending on the periods involved, you will need to provide details of your most recent periods of employment. List the companies, the exact period of employment, the nature of the positions you have held and your most recent salary.

### Credit information

You will be required to submit details of accounts you hold (savings, cheque, credit card), their account numbers, credit limits and your bank's name. If applicable, prepare details of bond/hire purchase/store accounts and other finance granted to you.

If applicable, prepare details of judgements taken out against you, sequestration/rehabilitation and convictions for criminal offences. Trying to hide such information from the banker is a bad idea. The bank will find out anyway, and the fact that you have not been truthful will count against you.

---

**Financial information**

List your current monthly income and state its sources. Also, prepare a list of your monthly expenses, including maintenance payments if applicable.

Prepare an up-to-date statement of assets and liabilities, including details of loans and repayment terms.

Prepare a schedule of contingent liabilities. (Contingent liabilities are potential liabilities. An example would be a surety you have signed in favour of someone else. If this person defaults, you will be called upon to pay.)

Draw up a list of insurance policies and state their surrender value.

---

## The business plan

*Planning is as natural to the process of success as its absence is to the process of failure.*

> Robin Sieger, British business executive

Several of the major commercial banks offer business plan templates. These packages can be downloaded from the banks' websites. On the upside, these packages are extremely user-friendly, and they are available either free of charge or at a highly subsidised price. On the downside, they tend to be less comprehensive than their commercially available counterparts, available on the Internet or from computer stores.

Some packages allow you to import figures created on a standard spreadsheet. Obtaining a package from the bank you plan to deal with has an additional advantage. The banker will be familiar with the layout of your business plan and this could count in your favour.

## Ten good reasons why a business plan is indispensable

1. Drafting a business plan forces you to think matters through in more detail than you otherwise would. This gives you a chance to identify potential problems early on and find a way around them.
2. The mere fact that you have taken the trouble to prepare a good business plan reflects careful analysis of the business's potential. This will provide you with the necessary peace of mind to drive your project forward with confidence.
3. The business plan will motivate other stakeholders to support the business. Stakeholders include funders, suppliers, customers, staff, business support agencies and the media.
4. The usefulness of a business plan endures well beyond the initial funding stage. If kept up to date, frequently referred to and used to track the direction the business takes, it will help you to spot problems early on. You can then deal with them before much damage has been done.
5. Regular review of the business plan necessitates the application of logical thought processes. This will have a positive impact on the quality of your management decisions.
6. Revision of the goals expressed in the business plan promotes lateral thinking among members of your team and facilitates the effectiveness of brainstorming sessions.
7. The business plan becomes a measurement and evaluation tool in the widest sense of the word. It can be used to determine which departments within your business have met or exceeded their goals. This creates benchmarks for investment decisions and performance appraisals.
8. The business plan facilitates staff buy-in through joint goal setting and progress tracking. This can be linked to the celebration of milestone events.
9. The business plan serves as an early-warning system for the identification of opportunities that may otherwise be overlooked. Once again, this facilitates the timely implementation of appropriate responses.
10. Although the business plan contains confidential information, it can nevertheless serve as a source document for the creation of press releases and other communications aimed at the business's constituency in the broadest sense.

*A business plan enables you to identify
potential problems early on*

### Contents of a business plan

Space limitations prevent us from providing detailed guidelines in this book. We will, however, list the headings you should cover.

- *Title sheet:* Put nothing on it except the name of the business, the words *Confidential Business Plan* and the date on which the plan was compiled. Your name and full contact details should be provided on the first inside page.

- *Contents page:* List all section headings and their relevant page numbers.

- *Executive summary:* This is arguably the most important portion of the business plan. Potential funders receive literally hundreds of business plans. If the summary is less than compelling, they may not even bother to read on.

- *Your business objectives:* Try to explain your objectives in a concise manner. Do not allow your imagination to run riot; rather stick to the facts.

- *The business concept:* Provide an in-depth picture of the business and its potential. Deal with the product, its sourcing or manufacture and the chain of supply. If appropriate, give details of your branding and packaging.

- *The market:* Describe your target market and why it will find your product irresistible. Under this heading, you should deal with market segmentation (the slice of the target market you wish to tackle first) and your competition.

- *The infrastructure:* Describe the infrastructure needed to serve your target market with optimal efficiency. Include premises, equipment, materials and staff.

Remember that your projections must tally with your sales forecasts for the forthcoming years. You would not want to be caught out having less capacity than your sales projections demand.

If you really want to knock them dead, mention at this point that your business processes will be documented in an operations manual. (Creating an operations manual as early as possible is a good idea anyway. It will help you to standardise processes, track implementation and ensure that your business complies with legal and statutory requirements. This will reduce wastage, enhance customer service levels and keep you on the right side of the law.)

- *The marketing mix:* Explain how you will market the business. This must tie in with statements about your target market you made earlier in this document.

- *Breakeven point:* The question 'How long will it take to reach breakeven?' will be on every potential investor's mind. Breakeven is the point when the business's income equals the sum total of costs and expenses. You could say that, at this point, the business operates in neutral. (You will find a formula for the calculation of your business's breakeven point later in this chapter, as well as in Chapter 3.)

- *You and your team:* Despite the advent of computers, business relationships continue to be built on effective relationships between people. Potential stakeholders will want to know who you are and what makes you tick. If you have partners and/or key personnel in the business, introduce them as well. Be realistic, but allow your passion to shine through.

- *The appendix:* Include financial projections, market research results and other documentation that supports the assumptions you have made. Copies of your vision and your mission statement should also be included.

You can delegate or outsource most tasks but the creation of your business plan is an exception. The plan must reflect your vision for the business and only you can create it!

## Financial projections

Your financial projections should consist of four documents, namely:

- sales forecast for at least three years
- pro forma income statement for at least one year
- pro forma balance sheet reflecting the situation of the business at least at the end of the first year
- cash flow projection for the first year.

*You need the right tools to do proper financial projections*

## Useful tools

Accountants have developed a series of tools that help users spot a business's strengths and weaknesses at a glance. They can be used in benchmarking exercises as well. Benchmarking means that you compare performance figures with those achieved by your competitors or published as industry standards. Not surprisingly, potential funders love them. For this reason, we list the most important ones below.

### Breakeven analysis

This is an extremely important tool. It enables you to assess when your business is trading in neutral. This means that trading activity covers all costs and expenses (total operating expenses) but creates no surplus (profit). You might think that this is not a very desirable position to be in, and you would be right. However, if you start a new business or add a new product line, patience is needed. Most new projects incur losses initially. Funders know and accept this, but like to be assured that breakeven point will be reached within a reasonable period going forward. The calculation is straightforward:

Breakeven sales = total operating expenses × 100 : gross profit percentage

### Current ratio

This ratio, also called the working capital ratio, expresses the business's ability to pay its current liabilities out of current assets. The formula is as follows:

Current assets : current liabilities

Current assets consist of stock, debtors and cash. Current liabilities consist of trade creditors and short-term loans. Interpretation of the resulting figure depends on the industry sector. As a general rule, a ratio of 2:1, meaning that for every rand you owe you have two rand in current assets to pay for it, is considered very good.

## Acid test ratio

This ratio is also known as the quick ratio. Its purpose is similar to that of the current ratio, except that it is more severe. The value of stock has been stripped out of the equation to provide a more realistic picture of a business's ability to meet its obligations in the short term. The formula is:

(Current assets – inventory) : current liabilities

## Stock turnaround ratio

This ratio measures the frequency at which stock, expressed in rand terms, is sold. The formula is:

Stock on hand (for resale purposes) : cost of sales for year to date × 365

A high frequency of stock turnaround means that stock moves rapidly through the business. This is desirable because little or no capital is tied up in obsolete stock.

## Debtors outstanding ratio

This ratio measures the number of days it takes you to collect outstanding debtors balances. The formula is:

Debtors at month end : credit sales for year to date × 365

This ratio is of enormous importance. You may have based your cash flow projections on the assumption that your customers adhere to your terms of 30 days net. The question is: Do they, or do they take significantly longer? If so, and you let it go unchecked, it can undermine your ability to meet your own obligations.

Ask your accountant to help you with the compilation of financial projections, but stay involved every step of the way. We mentioned earlier that if financial management is not your strong suit, now is the time to address this. Competition out there has become so intense that to operate a business successfully without a solid understanding of its financial well-being has become almost impossible.

## PACKAGE AND SELL YOUR PROJECT!

Why is it that some entrepreneurs find it easy to raise funds for their ventures whilst others fail? On occasion, the viability of the project may be suspect, but this is rarely the main problem. In far too many instances, it is the haphazard way in which a project is presented that puts paid to the entrepreneur's dreams.

*It is the haphazard way in which a project is presented that often kills an entrepreneur's dreams*

## Preparing a winning presentation

In essence, selling your project to investors is a marketing function and the techniques you should use are almost identical. Be careful, though – this is not a case of 'smoke and mirrors'! Just like any other marketing drive with long-term objectives, your quest for funding needs to be well researched, credible and aimed at creating win-win outcomes all-round.

### *Funders' expectations*

Before we go into the details of the presentation, let us define funders' expectations. Anyone you approach for finance will want to be assured that:

- you are an expert in your field
- you can handle money responsibly
- you are able to manage a business
- the product has proven potential
- the market segment you wish to enter is sound and on a sustainable growth curve.

Chances are that you have addressed most of these issues already. Still, you may find the following pointers useful.

### *Image considerations*

In theory, there is nothing stopping you from starting your business as a sole proprietor. This would mean that the business is unregistered and has no legal persona. However, our advice is: Avoid it if you can. We say this because it will not convey the right impression.

The establishment and operation of a company can be cumbersome and costly, but might be a funding requirement.

### *Demonstrating financial prudence*

There is a fine line between excessive spending and limiting spending to such an extent that it puts a lid on the business's growth potential. The following examples will illustrate this point:

- You want to start an advertising agency. To convey the right image, your financial projections should include an allowance for the rental of upmarket premises.

- A plumbing repair business, on the other hand, could – and should – place its administrative offices at a low-rental location.

- Similar considerations apply to vehicles. It is rarely necessary to drive the latest model of one of the top brands. In most instances, as long as a car is well maintained and in good running order, it will do the job.

> You will not impress your investors by telling them how you plan to blow their money on 'nice-to-haves'. A statement along the lines of 'we will go for all the bells and whistles once the business is making serious money' is much more likely to do that.

### **Playing to the audience**

Ask yourself: Who is most likely to give me the financial support I need? Then tailor your proposal to your target audience's expectations. Convincing a banker that you would administer a loan responsibly requires a different approach to attracting the interest of a venture capitalist. And the recruitment of a prospective working partner is another matter altogether.

This does not call for drastic changes to the basic documentation you have prepared. All it needs are slight adaptations to some portions of the core document. Some examples follow.

### Banker

A banker will want assurances that you will repay a loan, with interest, by the agreed time. And no matter how enlightened he or she may be, the amount of cash you plan to invest and what forms of security you offer remain important considerations. Top this off with a realistic cash flow projection that shows that you can make the repayments, including interest, and your loan should be in the bag.

### Venture capitalist

A venture capitalist's main objective is growth. He or she will be interested in the potential of your product and whether you have the necessary drive to maximise it. Provide detailed market research and competitor analyses. Above all, stress that because of your expertise and your passion for the business, high compound capital growth is virtually assured. End your proposal with an outline for a

*Ask yourself: Who is most likely to give me the financial support I need?*

realistic exit route for the venture capitalist five to seven years down the line and you should have a deal.

### *Working partner*

A prospective working partner will want to know how much money he or she is expected to inject. The solidity of the project, the type of work he or she is expected to perform and the level of decision-making power you grant will be other areas of concern. Convincing him or her that your project offers financial stability and job satisfaction should clinch the deal. (This is so important that it bears repeating: Unless true compatibility exists, going into partnership with someone can turn into a veritable nightmare. Do not do it unless you are certain that it is a match made in heaven.)

### *Government agency or nongovernmental organisation*

To obtain funding from these quarters, you need to convince the agency concerned that your project will create sustainable jobs and/or has distinct export potential.

## Face-to-face interviews

At some stage, you will have to meet with prospective funders in person. There is no need to be apprehensive. You have done your homework and you are ready to state your case.

Research suggests that the way we present ourselves has a significant impact. After all, first impressions are formed within the first 10 to 15 seconds of meeting someone new. To change these impressions may require several hours and you may never get a second chance.

Before you go into that all-important meeting, it is best to prepare for any eventuality. Regardless of whether you present to one banker or a room full of potential funders, the following pointers should prove useful:

*Prepare your presentation for the face-to-face interview*

- Prepare a professional-looking presentation, tailored to the needs of the target audience.

- Once you are truly happy with the contents of your presentation, practise its delivery until you are comfortable.

- The documentation you wish to hand out should be proofread, properly printed and bound. Should the meeting involve several people, establish their numbers in advance and prepare enough copies. Should you lack proper facilities, your local copy shop can help you with that. Remember: To make money you need to spend money first!

- Some people consider dress code an outdated notion, but do not be too hasty. It may be unfair to judge a book by its cover, but many people still do. Funders are people too. Unless you know the prevailing dress code, it is safer to err on the side of conservatism.

- Should you wish to use slides or a flip chart, arrange this in advance. Few things are worse than having a room full of people stare at you while you feverishly search for an extension cord.

- When you meet with a potential funder for the first time, make a point of being punctual. You should allow for the possibility of a traffic jam. Within reason, it is better to arrive early rather than late.

- Tailor your presentation to your audience's understanding of the topic and deliver it with passion. Unless you know that you are talking to a room full of industry experts, avoid technical jargon. Should this be impractical, explain every industry-specific term you use.

- Stress that you welcome questions. Answer them honestly and to the best of your ability. The mere fact that prospective funders ask questions indicates interest.

- If you do not know something, do not be afraid to say so. Offer to find out and come back to the questioner by a set date. Then make a point of doing just that.

At the end of the presentation, thank your audience members for their time and interest. Do this even if they show little inclination to back your project. It may not be a rejection. Perhaps your project does not fit in with their current investment strategy. They may even put you in touch with someone else, but this will not happen if you storm out in a huff.

## CONCLUSION

Once you have secured funding for your business start-up, it means that you have won the battle, not the war. Although congratulations are in order, the battle continues. Unless you operate in a sector where cash payments are the normal state of things, for example a fast-food outlet or home repair service, you will soon need additional funds to finance growth. As your business establishes itself, things do tend to become a little easier! There are several things you can do to speed up this process.

### Keep a tab on reality

As part of the work you did when you compiled your business plan, you created financial projections. The worst thing you could do at this point is to allow them to gather dust in your filing cabinet. Instead, you should use them to track progress.

If, for example, sales are below expectations or costs go through the roof, find out why. It could be that you overestimated the size of the market for one product. If so, find out what other products you could sell to the same market. And if this approach does not work, see which other markets may want to buy your original product. The point is that unless you know what is wrong, you cannot correct it.

> Make it a habit to monitor progress and adjust your plans accordingly.

### Keep people informed

You need to stay informed, and you need to let the right people know what is happening in your business as well. This way, developments will never take you by surprise. And when you need help at some point in the future, your associates will be more receptive.

*Make it a habit to monitor progress*

## Avoid overtrading

If, for example, sales are ahead of budget, it could turn out to be a mixed blessing. Celebrate your good fortune but then pull out your debtors age analysis and your cash flow projections. You may discover to your dismay that the more you sell the sooner you will run out of cash. Not because you are selling at a loss, but because your customers take longer to pay you than the terms your suppliers allow you. This is called *overtrading*. Unless you do something about it early on, your thriving business could go to the wall!

Do not wait until your suppliers threaten to close your account. Meet with them early on, explain what is happening, show them your projections and request extended credit. They want your business, so there is no reason why they should not oblige.

Deal with your banker in the same way. Do not wait until he or she bounces a cheque – this could mean the end of the road for your business. Keep in touch, provide regular progress reports and, if a cash crunch looms, speak up in time. Your banker, too, wants your business. As long as your situation looks stable, he or she will try to accommodate you.

## Create your personal brand

This is not a marketing book, so we are not talking about the branding of your business here. What we are suggesting is far more revolutionary and less understood. We are talking about enhancing your standing among your peers by creating your own personal brand.

Just think about it. If, through your actions, you establish yourself as a person who is not only knowledgeable in your chosen field but also forward-thinking, trustworthy and dependable, your name has the makings of a top brand. Market your personal brand appropriately and everyone, including your banker, will want to do business with you!

In his book *Build your own life brand* (Simon & Schuster, New York, 2002), American author and public speaker Stedman Graham proposes the following seven rules:

1. Your brand can't be all things to all people.

2. Keep stretching for everything within your grasp.

3. Think long term when building a life brand.

4. Market your brand but let it sell itself.

5. Fortify your brand by teaming up.

6. The strongest life brands are those that lift others up.

7. Build joy into your life brand.

We could not have put it better! Now start projecting, networking and winning! Most importantly, make it a habit to monitor progress.

# FINANCE FOR NON-FINANCIAL PEOPLE

*Kurt Illetschko*

## INTRODUCTION

For many people in business, and especially small businesses, finance and accounting are a complete mystery that they would rather hand over to their accountants.

Do not do that. Your accountant or bookkeeper is merely a scorekeeper. You actually need to know what is going on in your business yourself. You need to be able to 'read' your business, and the 'language' of business is accounting in the same way that mathematics is the 'language' of science.

The good news is: You do not need to become an accountant yourself. You merely need to be able to read financial statements, manage cash flow, create budgets and plan, and so on. All these things are perfectly simple to learn if we can just keep things in plain English.

You have to bear in mind that businesses do not operate in a vacuum. Private companies and close corporations (CCs) are governed by the Companies Act, Act 71 of 2008, and the Close Corporations Act of 1984 respectively. Since the implementation of the new Companies Act, no new

*Finance in your own business*

CCs can be registered, but existing CCs may continue trading indefinitely. The requirements regarding financial statements will be governed by the Companies Act. Please refer to Appendix 2.

Please also note that the Companies Act and the Close Corporations Act specify the roles and functions of directors of companies and of members of CCs. This information is freely available, so if you do things wrong you only have yourself to blame.

---

You can easily look up and download legislation and regulations relating to companies (or any other matter) from www.acts.co.za without having to pay anything. You can also search for specific words or phrases on the website.

Another very useful and user-friendly website that is absolutely crammed with facts is the website of the South African Revenue Service (SARS) at www.sars.gov.za. You can download a tax guide for small businesses that is updated annually from the site. It is easy to read and understand.

---

## FINANCIAL AND MANAGEMENT ACCOUNTS

### Introduction

The accounting needs of your business will vary according to its size, type and sector. As the business owner, it is your responsibility to make sure your business keeps accurate records and accounts.

There are two types of accounting information:

- financial accounts, which describe the performance of your business and have to be submitted to SARS.

*Make sure you know the difference between financial
and management accounting*

- management accounts, which are aimed at helping you plan your business and make decisions about key areas such as sales, margins and stock.

This chapter will explain the basics of both types of accounts and what they should include. It outlines your financial accounting obligations as well as how management accounting can help you run your business more effectively.

## Financial accounts

Financial accounts are a formal historical record of your business's performance over a past period (usually one year) for the benefit of external users, such as shareholders, employees, suppliers, bankers, tax authorities and, for larger companies, consumer groups.

Financial accounts normally include the following:

### Income statement

The income statement measures your business's performance over a given period of time, usually one year. It compares the income of your business with the cost of goods or services and expenses incurred in earning that revenue. (See pages 64 to 78.)

### Balance sheet

A balance sheet is a snapshot of your business's assets and liabilities on a particular day – usually based on your accounting year. (See pages 79 to 87.)

### Cash flow statement

A cash flow statement shows how your business has generated and disposed of cash and liquid funds. It also enables you to forecast the expected increases and decreases in cash flow over the coming year, which is critical in helping you identify any potential problems early on. (See pages 92 to 105.)

### Statement of changes in equity

This is an account of recognised gains and losses since the previous set of accounts, for example, changes caused by currency valuation, property revaluation, profits earned by associates and joint ventures not included in the normal accounts.

### Which businesses have to produce annual financial statements?

In terms of the Companies Act of 2008, if your business is a private company (limited liability company or Proprietary Limited) or CC, you must produce annual financial statements for each financial year.

Sole traders and most partnerships do not need to create formal financial accounts. They are required by SARS to maintain proper books and records to support annual income tax returns. These must be kept for a minimum period of six years.

However, there are numerous benefits to producing formal accounts, even if you are a sole trader or partner. If you are looking to grow your business, or need a loan or mortgage, or want to sell your business, for example, most institutions will ask to see three years' accounts.

### Preparing financial accounts of private companies and CCs

In terms of the Companies Act and Close Corporations Act, companies and CCs have to prepare and publish a set of financial accounts each year.

You must prepare accounts within 18 months of your business's formation, and thereafter within nine months of each financial year-end.

## Management accounts

Management accounts are invaluable in helping you to make timely and meaningful management decisions about your business.

Different businesses will have different management accounting needs, depending on the business areas that are important to them. These may include:

- the sales process, including pricing, distribution and debtors
- the purchasing process, including inventory records and creditors
- a fixed asset register
- employee records.

There is no legal requirement to prepare management accounts, but it is difficult to run a business effectively without them. Most companies produce them regularly, for example monthly or quarterly.

Although management accounts analyse recent historical performance, they are usually forward-looking with regard to elements such as sales, cash flow and profit forecasts. The analysis is usually performed against forecasts and budgets that are produced at the start of the year. See pages 106 to 116 for more information on how budgets can be used.

The information is usually broken down so that the performance of different elements of the business can be measured. For example, if a business has more than one outlet, there may be a separate report for each outlet. There may also be a report produced to show how well a particular product has done across different outlets.

*Make sure you know how to file your financial accounts*

### Uses of management accounting

Management accounts will enable you to:

- compare your accounts with original budgets or forecasts
- manage and focus your business better
- identify trends in your business
- highlight variations in your income or spending that may require attention.

They should be used for the following purposes:

### *Record keeping*

- recording business transactions
- measuring the results of financial changes
- projecting the financial effects of future transactions
- preparing internal reports in a user-friendly format.

### *Planning and control*

- collecting cash
- controlling inventory
- controlling expenses
- coordination and monitoring.

### *Decision making*

- using cost information for pricing, capital investment and marketing
- evaluating market and product profitability
- evaluating the financial effect of strategies and plans.

## THE INCOME STATEMENT

### Introduction

This section tells you about the basic financial records you need to keep to enable you to report your profit (or loss) each year. The information should help you decide whether you need the services of an accountant or bookkeeper, or whether you can do it yourself.

The income statement is a summary of business transactions for a given period – normally 12 months. By deducting total expenditure from total income, it shows on the 'bottom line' whether your business made a profit or loss at the end of that period.

The income statement is produced primarily for business purposes – to show owners, shareholders or potential investors how the business is performing, and is also submitted to SARS with your tax return to calculate your tax liability.

### Keeping accurate records

Whatever your type of business, by law you must keep accurate records of your income and expenditure. You

*Make sure you keep track of profits*

need to keep self-employment records for five years and company, CC or partnership records for six years after the latest date your tax return is due.

Accurate record keeping has important benefits. It:

- gives you the information you need to manage your business and make it grow

- enables you to report on your profit (or loss) easily and quickly when required

- will improve your chances of getting a loan or mortgage

- makes filling in your tax return easier and quicker

- helps you or your company avoid paying too much tax

- provides back-up for claims for certain allowances

- helps you plan and budget for tax payments

- prevents interest or penalties for late tax payments

- helps reduce fees if you use an accountant – your annual accounts will be far easier to produce.

The basic records you need to keep are:

- a list of all your sales and other income

- a list of all your expenditure, including day-to-day expenses and equipment

- a separate list for petty cash expenditure if relevant

- a record of goods taken for personal use and payments to the business for these

- back-up documents for all of the above.

You need the information above to create your income statement.

## Business income: sales

Business income falls into two categories for profit and loss reporting:

- sales or turnover

- other income.

For information on the second category, see the section that follows.

### *Business sales or turnover*

Your business's total sales of products and/or services in a trading year are referred to as turnover. This is the starting point for your income statement.

How you record sales will vary according to your business type and size. You may use a simple list or 'ledger' in a book, a tailored spreadsheet or a computer software

*You need lots and lots of sales documentation*

program. Whichever system you use, you need to ensure that it is accurate and updated regularly.

### Sales records back-up

The back-up records for your sales ledger fall into two categories and will vary according to your business type:

### *Sales documentation*

- copies of sales invoices issued by you

- rolls of till receipts

- delivery notes (proof of delivery).

### *Proof of income relating to the above*

- deposit slips

- bank statements

- if you operate on a 'cash only' basis you must keep detailed records of your income in your sales book or ledger and be able to relate these to your expenditure, cash in hand and bank statements.

## Business income: other

As well as reporting sales income, you need to report income to the business from other sources, for example:

- interest on business bank accounts

- sale of equipment you no longer need

- rental income to the business.

### Recording other income

- Record equipment sales on a separate schedule of assets.

- Keep a record of any rental income, for example if you sublet part of your office to someone else.

*You need to report the sale of equipment you no longer need*

### Back-up documentation

By law you must keep deposit slips and/or bank statements to account for your additional business income. Ideally, you should be able to cross-reference this documentation to the above 'other income' records.

## Recording business expenditure

Business expenditure falls into three key areas for the purpose of reporting your profit or loss. You can save yourself, or your accountant, time by grouping your costs accordingly in your purchase list or ledger. The three key areas are:

- cost of sales – the base cost of obtaining or creating your product

- business expenses (also called overheads)

- cost of equipment you have bought or leased for long-term use.

### Examples

The following example shows a simple income statement for a small service business with no cost of sales but some general expenses.

### Freelance Copywriting Service (sole proprietor)
### INCOME STATEMENT
### for the year ending 28 February 2011

|   |                          | 2011 R |
|---|--------------------------|-------:|
|   | **Income**               |        |
|   | Sales                    | 40 450 |
| 1 | Cost of sales            |      – |
| 2 | Gross profit             | 40 450 |
| 3 | Other income             |      – |
| 4 | Operating income         | 40 450 |
|   | **Expenses**             |        |
| 5 | Premises                 |    200 |
| 6 | Office costs             |    580 |
| 7 | Travel and subsistence   |     42 |
| 8 | Marketing and advertising|    475 |
| 9 | Depreciation             |    300 |
| 10| Total expenses           |  1 597 |
| 11| **Net profit before tax**| 38 853 |
| 12| **Tax**                  |    693 |
| 13| **Profit after tax**     | 38 160 |

**Notes**

1  Owner has no cost of sales; she simply writes material.

2  The gross profit is the sales less the cost of sales.

**3** In this case there is no other income.

**4** Since there is no cost of sales or other income, the operating income will be the same as the sales figure.

**5** The owner works at home. This is a proportionate part of the electricity cost.

**6** This includes stationery, post, telephone, Internet connection, toner and other office supplies.

**7** This is travel cost the owner could not reclaim from clients.

**8** The owner spent this money on web design and listings with search engines.

**9** The owner bought office furniture worth R1 200. She will deduct 25% per year of the value of this furniture over the next four years.

**10** This is the total of the owner's expenses, and is deducted from the gross profit.

**11** This is the amount left after the expenses are deducted from the gross profit.

**12** Tax is calculated using the statutory rates of tax for an individual – in this case 18% of profit, less a rebate of R6 300.

**13** This is the amount that the owner really made, i.e. the bottom line.

This example is of a small business with no cost of sales. The example on the following page shows a small business that does have cost of sales because products and parts as well as a service are supplied. It indicates the basis on which you decide whether a particular item is a cost of sale or an expense. Please note that tax rates, tax rebates and depreciation rates usually change annually. For this reason, the figures used in these calculations are examples only – the SARS website (www.sars.gov.za) provides current information.

Soweto Plumbing (Pty) Limited

| File ref. no. | Invoice or receipt date | Supplier | Description | VAT incl. | VAT (Note 3) | VAT excl. | How paid | Cost of sales (Note 1) | Travel | Car expenses | Interest on loan |
|---|---|---|---|---|---|---|---|---|---|---|---|
| | | | | | | | | | | General expenses (overheads) (Note 2) | |
| 001 | 23/05/11 | FNB | Loan interest on bakkie | 100 | – | 100 | Debit order | | | | 100 |
| 002 | 24/05/11 | The Pipe Co. | Plastic piping | 57 | 7 | 50 | Cash | 40,00 | | | |
| 003 | 25/05/11 | Soweto Building Supplies | Pump | 171 | 21 | 150 | Credit card | 120,00 | | | |
| 004 | 26/05/11 | Engen petrol station | Petrol | 68 | 0 | 68 | Petrol card | | | 68 | |
| 005 | 27/05/11 | Wesbank | Bakkie insurance | 228 | 28 | 200 | Internet transfer | | | 200 | |

**Note 1**

The items that one should include under 'cost of sales' will depend on the type of business you are in. In this case it is a plumbing service, so the supplied parts (pipes, pump) are a cost of sale. In a retail shop the stock bought will be a cost of sale. If you are a small manufacturer of goods, for example a furniture maker, cost of sales will include tools used as well as labour costs of people you employ to manufacture the product.

**Note 2**

Other items that Soweto Plumbing may include under general expenses or overheads are: telephone, stationery, repairs and maintenance, finance charges, legal costs, rental, electricity, water and rates, cell phones, computer costs, etc.

**Note 3**

Depending on the nature of the expense, value-added tax (VAT) can either be claimed back from SARS (input VAT) or it forms part of the cost of the item as SARS does not allow VAT on that item to be claimed back. Generally, most business-related expenses include VAT and can be claimed back on your VAT return. However, certain items, such as petrol, interest paid, and lease or hire purchase agreement repayments, cannot be claimed on your VAT return.

### *Business expenditure back-up*

The back-up records for your business expenditure fall into two categories. As with sales records, they will vary according to your business type.

### *Purchase/expenditure documentation*

- copies of supplier invoices/receipts issued to you

- till receipts for items bought over the counter

- payroll if you have employees.

### Proof of expenditure relating to the above

- cheque book stubs
- bank statements
- credit card statements and receipts.

It is important for you to be able to cross-reference your records to your expenditure figures if asked. If you mislay a receipt for a small item, make sure you enter it in your purchase or petty cash book ledger and make a note that you have lost the receipt.

The following example shows the income statement for a small company manufacturing and supplying gifts. Note especially the treatment of the cost of sales.

**Sample Design CC**
**INCOME STATEMENT**
**for the year ending 28 February 2011**

|   |   | 2011 R |
|---|---|---|
|   | **Income** |   |
|   | Sales | 140 450 |
|   | Cost of sales |   |
| 1 | Opening stock | 1 250 |
| 2 | Purchases | 18 500 |
| 3 | Less: Closing stock | (1 000) |
| 4 |   | 18 750 |
| 5 | Labour production cost | 28 000 |
|   |   | 46 750 |
|   | Gross profit | 93 700 |
| 6 | Other income | 50 |
|   | Operating income | 93 750 |

|   | **Expenses** | |
|---|---|---:|
|   | Travel | 400 |
|   | Motor car | 100 |
|   | Marketing | 750 |
|   | Office administration | 1 500 |
| **7** | Depreciation | 4 000 |
| **8** | Salaries and other staff costs | 12 000 |
| **9** | Members' remuneration | 50 000 |
|   | Total expenses | 68 750 |
|   | **Net profit before tax** | **25 000** |
|   | **Tax @ 30%** | **7 500** |
|   | **Net profit after tax** | **17 500** |

**Notes**

1  The opening stock consists of the value of stock and raw materials carried over from the previous year.

2  This is the total value of the raw materials bought to make the products.

3  This is the value of remaining materials not used up by year-end. It is a negative expense, i.e. an asset. It will appear as an expense in the next year's accounts under opening stock.

4  This is the cost of stock sold during the year, i.e. the difference between what the company started off with and bought, and what it is left with (opening stock plus purchases less closing stock).

5  This was the cost of paying production staff and a team of self-employed home workers to hand-paint the gifts. It is part of the cost of sales because this was a labour cost incurred in the course of manufacturing the product.

6  The company sold an old computer for R50 so it had to show this as other income.

**7** The company has decided to spread the cost of machinery of R16 000 over four years at 25% per year.

**8** This is the cost of a full-time half-day assistant.

**9** This is basically what the members are paying themselves as a salary. This cost, as well as the cost under point 8, are shown as expenses, not as costs of sales, because they are not directly associated with the manufacturing of the product.

## Cost of sales

The cost of sales is the base cost of obtaining or creating your product.

This may include:

- the cost of stock you buy for resale
- labour to produce the product
- machine hire
- small tools
- other production costs.

When you create your income statement, you deduct your cost of sales from your overall sales (turnover) to arrive at your 'gross profit'. This is your profit before the deduction of expenses or overheads.

Cost of sales does not usually apply if you supply a service only.

## Business expenses (overheads)

These are all the ongoing expenses associated with running your business that you can deduct from your 'profit before taxation' figure on your income statement.

Legitimate business expenses for accounting purposes are:

- employee costs
- premises costs
- repairs

- general administration
- motor expenses
- travel/subsistence
- advertising/promotion/entertainment
- interest
- bad debts
- legal/professional costs
- other finance charges
- depreciation or loss (profit) on sales of equipment
- any other expenses.

Note that some elements of these expenses are not allowed for tax purposes and are added back before your taxable profit is calculated.

*Don't overdo the business expenses*

## Cost of equipment

Any items of equipment you have bought or leased for long-term use are called capital items or fixed assets, and the expense is known as capital expenditure or simply capex for short. These may include:

- furniture

- computer equipment

- vehicle (car, bakkie, van) necessary for the business

- machinery

- premises.

Capital items cannot be deducted from your taxable profits in the same way as expenses. However, you still need to keep accurate records because you can spread the costs over several accounting years in your income statement. You may also be able to claim allowances against your net profit for a percentage of the cost of the item.

Depending on the size of your business, you can record the cost of equipment you buy in a separate register of equipment (the fixed asset register), or you can include it in your general expenditure records and show it as a capital item.

## Accounting periods and financial years

For the purposes of an income statement, accounting periods and financial years vary depending on the type of business in question.

### Accounting periods for the self-employed and partnerships

Self-employed and partnership accounts are set to 28 February each year to coincide with the tax year as regulated by tax legislation. If you keep to this date you may need to produce accounts for a part-year to start with, but it will save you time in the long run.

### Accounting periods for CCs and private companies

CCs and private companies can make their accounts up to any date. The accounting period is also referred to as the company's financial year. A normal accounting period will be 12 months, but sometimes it can be shorter – for example where a company started business in the middle of the year, but wants its financial year to end on 31 December.

*Financial terminology can be complicated, but it is important that you master the basics*

# THE BALANCE SHEET

## Introduction

A balance sheet is a financial account at a given point in time. It provides a snapshot summary of what a business owns or is owed (assets) and what it owes (liabilities).

The balance sheet shows how the business is being funded and how those funds are being used.

The balance sheet is used in three ways:

- for reporting purposes as part of a private company or CC's annual accounts

- to help you and other interested parties such as investors, creditors or shareholders assess the worth of your business at a given moment

- as a tool to help you analyse and improve the management of your business.

This section explains who needs to produce balance sheets and when, the different elements within them and how to use the information from a balance sheet to assess and manage business performance.

## Balance sheet reporting – the basics

Companies and CCs must produce a balance sheet as part of their annual accounts for submission to SARS and to shareholders.

In addition to the balance sheet, annual accounts include the following:

- income statement

- auditor's reports or independent review (if required – see Appendix 1)

- directors' report

- notes to the accounts.

Other parties who may wish to see the accounts – and therefore the balance sheet – include:

- potential lenders or investors

- potential purchasers of the business

- government departments carrying out inspections

- managers and trade unions.

### Reporting requirements for other business structures

Self-employed people and partners are not required to submit audited financial statements with their tax return. However, SARS requires the relevant financial details to be entered in a set format, so you may find it beneficial to prepare the figures in a balance sheet format.

*If things do not balance in a balance sheet
there is something wrong*

There are other key benefits of producing a balance sheet:

- If you want to raise finance, most lenders or investors will want to see three years' accounts.

- If you want to bid for large contracts, including government contracts, the client will want to see audited accounts.

- Producing audited accounts – including a balance sheet – will help you monitor the performance of your business.

- If you want to sell your business, it is almost impossible to do so without audited accounts.

## Contents of the balance sheet

A balance sheet shows:

- fixed assets – what the business owns
- current assets – what the business is owed
- current liabilities – what the business owes and must repay in the short term
- long-term liabilities – what the business owes and must repay in the long term, including the owners' capital.

A balance sheet balances because its assets always have the same value as its liabilities – what is owed to its owners (capital and profits) and what is owed to others (suppliers, lenders, SARS, etc.).

### Fixed assets

Fixed assets include:

- tangible assets, for example buildings, land, machinery, computers, fixtures and fittings (where relevant shown at their depreciated or resale value)

- intangible assets, for example goodwill, intellectual property rights, patents, trademarks, website domain names and long-term investments.

### Current assets

Current assets are short-term assets whose value can fluctuate from day to day, and can include:

- stock
- work in progress
- money owed by customers
- cash in hand or at the bank
- short-term investments
- pre-payments, for example advance rents.

A fixed asset in one business may be a current asset in another. For example, a computer is a fixed asset in most businesses, but most computers in a store selling computers are current assets. Only computers used by staff are fixed assets in such a case.

### Current liabilities

These are amounts owing and due within one year, and can include:

- money owed to suppliers
- short-term loans, overdrafts or other finance
- taxes due within the year, i.e. VAT and Pay as You Earn (PAYE)
- company tax.

**ABC (Pty) Limited**
**BALANCE SHEET**
**as at 28 February 2011**

|  |  | 2011 R |
|---|---|---|
|  | **ASSETS** |  |
| 1 | **Non-current assets** |  |
|  | Property, plant and equipment | 500 000 |
|  | **Current assets** | 785 000 |
| 2 | Accounts receivable | 350 000 |
| 3 | Inventory | 245 000 |
| 4 | Investments | 90 000 |
| 5 | Cash at bank and on hand | 100 000 |
|  | **Total assets** | **1 285 000** |
|  | **EQUITY AND LIABILITIES** |  |
|  | **Capital and reserves** | 201 000 |
| 6 | Share capital | 1 000 |
| 7 | Retained income | 200 000 |
|  | **Non-current liabilities** | 404 000 |
| 8 | Shareholders loans | 54 000 |
| 9 | Interest-bearing borrowings | 350 000 |
|  | **Current liabilities** | 680 000 |
| 10 | Accounts payable | 400 000 |
| 11 | Current portion of interest-bearing borrowings | 135 000 |
| 12 | Bank overdraft | 145 000 |
|  | **Total equity and liabilities** | **1 285 000** |

**Notes**

**1**   This is the cost of business premises, furniture and equipment, and machinery, less depreciation charged since first using the assets.

**2**   This is the total amount that customers owe, less bad debts and amounts considered uncollectible.

**3**   Inventory or stock is the total amount of goods bought from suppliers that have not yet been sold, plus raw materials held for production, plus the value of work in progress.

**4**   These are investments held by the company, e.g. money held in a money-market unit trust.

**5**   This is the total cash held at the site itself plus the balance in the company's current account with the bank.

**6**   These are the funds invested by the owners of the business, e.g. to finance its assets.

**7**   These are the profits made since the start of the business less expenses and amounts paid to the owners as dividends.

**8**   Same as point 6, but in this case the shareholders provided the funds in the form of a loan.

**9**   This is money borrowed from third parties like banks to fund assets or working capital repayable over a period of more than one year.

**10**   This is the total of the amounts paid by the business to its suppliers for goods it bought to sell to its customers.

**11**   This is the portion of the business's bank loan that is due to be repaid in less than one year.

**12**   This is when a company arranges to borrow money from its bank by taking out more money than it has in its account. An overdraft can be cancelled at any time by the bank and is therefore potentially an amount that has to be repaid in the short term.

### *Long-term liabilities*

These include:

- creditors due after one year – loans or financing due to be repaid after one year, for example bank or directors' loans and finance agreements

- capital and reserves – share capital and retained profits, after dividends.

## Interpreting balance sheet figures

A balance sheet is designed to show:

- how affluent the business is
- how liquid its assets are (liquid assets are in the form of cash or can easily be converted into cash)
- how the business is financed
- how much capital is being used.

Be aware that the figures include an element of judgement and can change dramatically in the space of a few hours.

### Current liabilities (money you owe in the short term)

This section may include interest due on loans. If interest rates rose sharply, this figure would instantly be out of date.

*Interpreting a balance sheet can be hard*

With a large loan and tight cash flow, a business may even become insolvent.

### Debtors (money owed to you)

This figure assumes that the debtors will pay up when the time comes, but there is always a chance that some of them may not.

### Property, plant and equipment

These are fixed assets and shown at their depreciated rates. There are two main approaches to calculating depreciation of an asset. In considering both cases, you should take into account the original value of the asset, the estimated lifespan of the asset and any remaining value.

The first approach involves writing off the same charge over the calculated life of the asset. For example, you may decide that a computer bought for R5 000 has a useful life of five years and that you will write off 20% of its value each year.

The second approach is to apply a steeper depreciation rate in the first few years of an asset's value. For example, you may decide to offset 30% of the value of the same computer in the first two years, 20% in the third year and 10% in the final two years. This method may allow your business to keep pace with trends in the market value of the asset.

Depreciation costs must be realistic and you may wish to approach your accountant for further help. The rates of depreciation that are allowable for various types of assets for tax purposes are determined by SARS from time to time.

## Accounting periods

A balance sheet normally reflects a business's position on the last day of its accounting period. An accounting period, also called the financial year, is usually 12 months but can be shorter or longer in the first year of trading.

## Internal accounts

Your business should draw up accounts frequently. Most businesses do so at least monthly. A monthly review of your internal accounts helps you to monitor business performance. In this case, the figures – often known as management accounts – are for internal use only. You do not need to file them with SARS. SARS only needs to see your financial statements once a year.

# INTERPRETING THE FINANCIAL INFORMATION

## Relationship between balance sheet and income statement

*The income statement summarises a business's trading transactions* – income, sales and expenditure – and the resulting profit or loss for a given period.

*The balance sheet, by comparison, provides a financial snapshot at a given moment.* It does not show day-to-day transactions or the current profitability of the business. However, many of its figures relate to or affect the state of play with income statement transactions on a given date.

The income statement feeds any profits not paid out as dividends into the retained income column shown on the balance sheet.

If the business takes out a short-term loan, this will be reflected in the balance sheet under current liabilities, but the loan itself will not appear in the income statement.

However, the income statement will include interest payments on that loan in its expenditure column – and these figures will affect the bottom line.

## Analysing balance sheets to assess business performance

Many of the standard measures used to assess the financial health of a business involve comparing figures on the balance sheet with those on the income statement.

There are some simple balance sheet comparisons you can make to assess the strength or performance of your business against earlier periods, or against direct competitors. The figures you study will vary according to the nature of the business. Some comparisons draw on figures from the income statement.

### *Internal comparisons*

If *inventory* (stock) levels on your balance sheet are rising from one period to the next, but sales in your income statement are not, some of your stock may be out of date or unsaleable. You may also have a cash flow problem developing.

If the amount owed to you by *trade debtors* is growing faster than sales, it could indicate poor internal credit control. You may want to find out whether there are customers who are having problems and could pose a threat to your business.

Nurturing a positive relationship with your *trade creditors* (companies you owe money to) is essential. Key to this is managing your cash flow well so that you can pay them on time. Trade creditors are more likely to be flexible about extending terms of credit if you have built up a good payment record.

Making early payments may qualify you for a discount. However, early payment for the sake of it will impact negatively on your cash flow. Good payment controls will help prevent imbalances in what you owe suppliers and levels of stock and inventory.

Borrowing as a percentage of overall financing (also known as 'gearing') is important – the lower the figure, the stronger your business is financially. It is common for start-up businesses to have high borrowing requirements, but if the figure reaches 50% you are likely to have difficulty getting further loans.

### External comparisons

You can also compare the above balance sheet figures with those of direct or successful competitors to see how you

*You need to compare balance sheets to assess
business performance*

measure up. This exercise will highlight weaknesses in your business operation that may need attention. It will also confirm strong business performance.

## Using accounting ratios to assess business performance

Ratio analysis is a good way for you to evaluate the financial results of your business in order to gauge its performance.

Ratios can be more helpful than the use of raw statistics. They provide you with the means of comparing your business against different standards by demonstrating the relationship between two figures on your business's balance sheet. This enables you to compare your own business, for example, against industry standards.

There are four main methods of ratio analysis – liquidity, solvency, efficiency and profitability.

### *Liquidity ratios*

There are three types of liquidity ratios:

- The *current ratio* (or working capital ratio) is current assets divided by current liabilities. This broadly gauges your business's financial health and assesses whether you have sufficient assets to cover your liabilities. An acceptable ratio for this is 2, indicating that you have twice as many current assets as current liabilities.

- The *quick or acid test ratio* is current assets (excluding stock) divided by current liabilities. This ratio excludes stock and measures a business's liquid assets compared to its liabilities. A ratio of 1 in this category indicates that liquidity levels are high – this is an indication of solid financial health. The reason stock is excluded in this ratio is that stock is often difficult to turn into cash in the short term.

- The *defensive interval* is quick assets divided by daily operating expenses. This gauges the threat of insolvency by measuring the number of days your business can survive without cash coming in. This should be between 30 and 90 days.

### Solvency ratios

*Gearing* (also known as the interest coverage ratio) is the ratio obtained by dividing loans and bank overdraft by equity and long-term loans and bank overdraft. This is expressed as a percentage and is a sign of solvency.

The higher the gearing, the more vulnerable the company is to increases in interest rates. Most lenders will refuse further finance if gearing exceeds 50%. However, some small start-up businesses may find that their gearing is higher than this percentage.

### Efficiency ratios

There are three types of efficiency ratios:

- *Debtors turnover* is sales (including VAT) divided by debtors. The ratio is divided into days of the year, indicating the average collection period and how effective your business's payment terms are. A low ratio indicates that payment terms may need tightening up or that debt collection is proving difficult. Both of these will have a negative knock-on effect on cash flow. The average debt collection should normally not exceed 30 days, but this period may vary enormously depending on the industry sector you are in.

- *Creditors turnover* is cost of sales divided by creditors. This ratio is divided into days of the year, indicating the average payment period, i.e. how long your business takes to pay suppliers. Suppliers may withdraw credit if you do not pay them on time.

- *Stock turnover* is cost of sales divided by stock level. This ratio is divided into the days of the year, indicating the average holding period. The speed of stock turnover varies by industry, but a lower stock turnover generally means lower profits and worse cash flow.

### Profitability ratios

This method involves calculating profit before income tax as a percentage of total capital employed. It indicates how well you can produce returns on the capital used in your business. This can then be compared to what the same amount of money (loans and shares) would have earned on deposit or in the stock market.

## CASH FLOW MANAGEMENT

### Introduction

Cash is the oxygen that enables a business to survive and prosper, and is the primary indicator of business health. While a business can survive for a short time without sales or profits, without cash it will die. For this reason the inflow and outflow of cash needs careful monitoring and management.

This section looks at the key elements of cash flow and at how cash flow management will help protect the financial security of your business. It outlines the steps that you can take when dealing with your customers, suppliers and stakeholders to improve cash flow. It also highlights common cash flow problems and how to avoid them.

## All about cash flow

Cash is the measure of your ability to pay your bills on a regular basis. This, in turn, depends on the timing and amount of cash flowing into and out of the business each week and month – your cash flow.

Cash includes:

- coins and notes

- current accounts and short-term deposits

- bank overdrafts and short-term loans

- foreign currency and deposits that can quickly be converted into rands.

*Make sure your cash flow does not only go one way*

Cash does not include:

- long-term deposits
- long-term borrowing
- money owed by customers
- stock.

### Difference between cash and profit

It is important not to confuse cash with profit. Profit is the difference between the total amount your business earns and all of its costs, usually assessed over a year or other trading period. You may be able to forecast a good profit for the year, yet still face times when you are strapped for cash. For instance, you may invoice a large sum, but if the customer does not pay the invoice, no cash comes in, and yet you still have to pay your salaries and your suppliers.

### Cash is king

To make a profit, most businesses have to produce and deliver goods or services to their customers before being paid. Unfortunately, no matter how profitable the contract, if you do not have enough money to pay your staff and suppliers before receiving payment, you will be unable to deliver your side of the bargain or receive any profit.

To trade effectively and be able to grow your business, you need to build up cash reserves by ensuring that the timing of cash movements puts you in an overall positive cash flow situation.

## Cash inflows and cash outflows

Ideally, during the business cycle, you will have more money flowing in than flowing out. This will allow you to build up cash reserves with which to plug cash flow gaps, seek expansion and reassure lenders and investors about the health of your business.

You should note that income and expenditure cash flows rarely occur together, with inflows often lagging behind. Your aim must be to do all that you can to speed up the inflows and slow down the outflows.

### Cash inflows

- payment for goods or services from your customers

- receipt of a bank loan

- interest on savings and investments

- shareholder investments.

### Cash outflows

- purchase of stock, raw materials or tools

- wages, rent and daily operating expenses

- purchase of fixed assets, for example computers, machinery, office furniture, etc.

- loan repayments

- dividend payments

- income tax, corporation tax, VAT and other taxes.

Many of your regular cash outflows, such as salaries, loan repayments and tax, have to be made on fixed dates. You must always be in a position to meet these payments, to avoid large fines or a disgruntled workforce.

To improve everyday cash flow you can:

- ask your customers to pay sooner

- use factoring (getting a third party to buy your invoices)

- ask for extended credit terms with suppliers

- negotiate the right deals with suppliers

- order less stock but more often

- lease rather than buy equipment.

You can also improve cash flow by increasing borrowing, or putting more money into the business. This is acceptable for coping with short-term downturns or to fund growth in line with your business plan, but should not form the basis of your cash strategy.

## The principles of cash flow forecasting

Cash flow forecasting enables you to predict peaks and troughs in your cash balance. It helps you to plan borrowing and tells you how much surplus cash you are likely to have at a given time. Many banks require forecasts before considering a loan.

*Ask your customers to pay sooner*

### Elements of a cash flow forecast

The cash flow forecast identifies the sources and amounts of cash coming into your business, and the destinations and amounts of cash going out over a given period. There are normally two columns listing forecast and actual amounts respectively.

The forecast is usually done for a year or quarter in advance and divided into weeks or months. It is best to pick periods during which most of your fixed costs – such as salaries – go out. The forecast lists:

- receipts

- payments

- excess of receipts over payments, with negative figures shown in brackets

- opening bank balance

- closing bank balance.

It is important to base initial sales forecasts on realistic estimates. If you have an established business, an acceptable method is to combine sales revenues for the same period 12 months earlier with predicted growth.

### Accounting software

Accounting software will help you prepare your cash flow forecast, allowing you to update your projections if there is a change in market trends or your business fortunes. Planning for seasonal peaks and troughs is simplified, and you can also make 'what-if' calculations.

## Cash flow forecast: ABC (Pty) Limited
## June 2011 to December 2011

| Month | 06/11 | 07/11 | 08/11 | 09/11 | 10/11 | 11/11 | 12/11 |
|---|---|---|---|---|---|---|---|
| Opening bank balance | 200 000 | 617 452 | 653 465 | 683 560 | 722 006 | 760 453 | 693 528 |
| **INFLOWS** | | | | | | | |
| Sales | 938 217 | 951 352 | 951 352 | 965 623 | 965 623 | 965 623 | 1 219 683 |
| **OUTFLOWS** | | | | | | | |
| Purchases | 394 573 | 789 147 | 795 065 | 800 984 | 800 984 | 906 355 | 903 019 |
| Accounting fees | 3 000 | 3 000 | 3 000 | 3 000 | 3 000 | 3 000 | 3 000 |
| Bank charges | 4 000 | 4 000 | 4 000 | 4 000 | 4 000 | 4 000 | 4 000 |
| Safety and security | 800 | 800 | 800 | 800 | 800 | 800 | 800 |
| Rental equipment | 3 000 | 3 000 | 3 000 | 3 000 | 3 000 | 3 000 | 3 000 |
| Water and electricity | 7 000 | 7 000 | 7 000 | 7 000 | 7 000 | 7 000 | 7 000 |
| Rent | 15 000 | 15 000 | 15 000 | 15 000 | 15 000 | 15 000 | 15 000 |
| Telephone and fax | 3 000 | 3 000 | 3 000 | 3 000 | 3 000 | 3 000 | 3 000 |
| Insurance | 2 500 | 2 500 | 2 500 | 2 500 | 2 500 | 2 500 | 2 500 |

| | | | | | | |
|---|---|---|---|---|---|---|
| Wages | 25 000 | 25 000 | 25 000 | 25 000 | 25 000 | 50 000 |
| Sundry expenses | 4 500 | 4 500 | 4 500 | 4 500 | 4 500 | 4 500 |
| Cleaning expenses | 1 000 | 1 000 | 1 000 | 1 000 | 1 000 | 1 000 |
| Vehicle expenses | 2 000 | 2 000 | 2 000 | 2 000 | 2 000 | 2 000 |
| Uniforms | 300 | 300 | 300 | 300 | 300 | 300 |
| Advertising and promotion | 3 000 | 3 000 | 3 000 | 3 000 | 3 000 | 3 000 |
| **Loan repayment** | 52 092 | 52 092 | 52 092 | 52 092 | 52 092 | 52 092 |
| **TOTAL OUTFLOWS** | 915 339 | 921 258 | 927 176 | 927 176 | 1 032 548 | 1 054 212 |
| Closing bank balance | 653 465 | 683 560 | 722 006 | 760 453 | 693 528 | 858 999 |

*(First data column: TOTAL OUTFLOWS 520 766, Closing bank balance 617 452)*

## Notes

- The opening bank balance plus the cash that flowed in, less the cash that flowed out, equals the closing bank statement, which is always the same as the opening bank statement of the following month.
- The cash flow forecast period could be any period; it just depends on circumstances. Annual cash flow forecasts that go with the budget are common though.
- Note that all forecast figures must relate to sums that are due to be collected and paid out, not to invoices sent and received. The forecast is a live entity. It will need adjusting in line with long-term changes to actual performance or market trends.

## Managing income and expenditure

Effective cash flow management is as critical to business survival as providing services or products. Below are some of the key methods to help reduce the time gap between expenditure and receipt of income.

### Customer management

- Define a credit policy that clearly sets out your standard payment terms.

- Issue invoices promptly and regularly chase outstanding payments. Use an 'aged debtor list' to keep track of invoices that are overdue and monitor your performance in receiving payments.

- Consider exercising your right to charge penalty interest for late payment.

- Consider offering discounts for prompt payment.

- Negotiate deposits or staged payments for large contracts. It is in your customers' interest that you do not go out of business trying to meet their demands.

- Consider using a third party to buy your invoices in return for a percentage of the total. This process is known as invoice discounting or factoring. It is a bit complex and expensive but can generate cash for you in difficult circumstances.

### Supplier management

- Ask for extended credit terms.

- Giving your suppliers incentives such as large or regular orders may help, but make sure you have a market for the orders you are placing.

- Consider reducing stock levels and using just-in-time systems.

### Taxation
VAT can be a huge short-term drain on cash. Unlike other creditors, SARS is not willing to wait. Make sure that you consider the effect of VAT on your cash flow.

### Asset management
Consider leasing fixed assets (equipment) or buying them on hire purchase. Buying outright can result in a huge drain on cash in the first year of business.

## Cash flow problems and how to avoid them
No matter how effective your negotiations with customers and suppliers, poor business practices can put your cash flow at risk.

Look out for:

- *Poor credit control:* Failure to run credit checks on your customers is a high-risk strategy, especially if your debt collection is inefficient.

*Watch out for cash flow problems*

- *Failure to fulfil your order:* If you do not deliver on time or to specification you will not get paid. Implement systems to measure production efficiency and the quantity and quality of stock you hold and produce.

- *Ineffective marketing:* If your sales are stagnating or falling, revisit your marketing plan. Are you targeting your customers properly or is one sales executive bringing in all the business?

- *Inefficient ordering service:* Make it easy for your customers to do business with you. Encourage them to send orders by fax or e-mail or to phone them in – the postal system is too slow and unreliable. Ensure that catalogues and order forms are clear and easy to use.

- *Poor management accounting:* Keep an eye on key accounting ratios that will alert you to an impending cash flow crisis or prevent you from taking orders you cannot handle.

- *Inadequate supplier management:* Your suppliers may be overcharging or taking too long to deliver. Create a supplier management system.

### Cash management in action: a case study

The following simple example shows how a small, profitable business can run into unforeseen cash flow problems when it takes on a new large order.

Wondagifts is a small but profitable gift designer and supplier with three full-time staff (including the two owners). It outsources production, but supplies the raw materials itself to save on costs. It then finishes and packages the final product on site.

Wondagifts does not have any loans or overdrafts. It has a long-term customer base of small gift shops and visitor centres.

Wondagifts suddenly wins a large order to supply specially designed wall decorations for a chain of stores. The contract promises to double its turnover.

The team takes on an additional employee and works flat out to meet the deadlines. It does not notice an impending cash flow crisis resulting from a fall in repeat orders from existing customers combined with a jump in raw material costs.

To make matters worse, the new client keeps changing its mind about designs. A misunderstanding means that the first run of goods is rejected, causing a delay in payment and increased production costs. Wondagifts orders additional materials to make up the shortfall in the run.

*Make sure you know how to order efficiently*

By the time the order is complete, Wondagifts is running an expensive overdraft. Profit margins have been squeezed to the limit and it has lost several of its existing customers. A downturn in the fortunes of the retail chain means that it does not place any further orders.

After a lot of hard work, Wondagifts finds itself back where it was five years earlier.

Tighter cash flow management would have highlighted the fall in repeat orders and rise in raw material costs. Wondagifts would also have benefited from a client contract that included:

- milestone payments and penalty provisions for changes such as those in the designs, for example increased fees

- sharing the cost of additional materials with the new client or getting the client to pay for them.

## Refinements to a simple cash flow forecast

There is no single best way to set out a cash flow forecast. Some refinements to the most basic ways of setting out the information will give you a more sophisticated view of your business's situation.

You could, for example, separate cash flow for business operations from funding cash flow. This gives a clearer picture of the actual performance of your business and is a format that many accountants prefer.

### Cash flow from operations

This includes inflows such as:

- cash sales

- receipts from credit sales in earlier periods

- interest on savings.

It includes outflows such as:

- payments to suppliers
- hire purchase and lease payments
- expenses such as rent, rates, insurance, water and electricity and telephone
- wages or salaries
- taxes
- interest on loans and bank charges.

### Funding cash flows

This includes inflows such as:

- loans from banks
- increase in share capital.

It includes outflows such as:

- dividends paid
- loans repaid.

With these two types of cash flow separated, you can gauge how self-sufficient the day-to-day working of your business is. A net outflow in operational cash flow is usually an indicator of problems that need to be addressed quickly.

# BUDGETING AND BUSINESS PLANNING

## Introduction

Once your business is operational, it is essential to plan and tightly manage its financial performance. In order to cover your bills while developing the business, you will need to know when you are likely to receive revenue and incur costs.

Creating a budgeting process is the most effective way to keep the business – and its finances – on track.

This section outlines the advantages of business planning and budgeting, and explains how to go about it. It suggests action points to help you manage your business's financial position more effectively and ensure your plans are practical.

## Annual business planning

Once you have started trading, it is easy to get immersed in day-to-day problem solving, dealing with cash flow issues and challenges as they arise. However, it is worth

*Forecasting can be a tricky business*

investing some time creating and managing budgets and regularly reviewing your business plan. This can help keep the money moving smoothly – allowing you to concentrate on growing your business.

The most successful businesses use structured planning to make the most of key areas, including:

- revenue growth
- return on sales
- assets and equity.

Many businesses carry out – almost on a daily basis – the majority of the activities associated with business planning, such as thinking about growth areas, competitors, cash flow and profit.

Converting this into a cohesive process to manage your business's development does not have to be difficult or time-consuming. The most important thing is that you make plans that are dynamic and are communicated to everyone involved.

### Benefits of annual business planning

The key benefit is that it gives you the opportunity to stand back and review your business performance and the factors affecting your business. Other benefits include:

- a better ability to make continuous improvements
- a greater ability to anticipate problems
- sound financial information on which to base decisions
- improved clarity and focus
- greater confidence in your decision making.

## Components of an annual plan

The main aim of your annual business plan is to set out the strategy and action plan for your business. This should include a clear financial picture of where you stand – and where you expect to stand – over the coming year.

Your annual business plan should include:

- an outline of changes that you want to make to your business

- potential changes to your market, customers and competition

- your objectives and goals for the year

- your key performance indicators

- any issues or problems

- any operational changes

- your management and people

- your financial performance and forecasts

- investment in the business.

Business planning is most effective when it is an ongoing process. This allows you to act quickly where necessary, rather than simply reacting to events after they have happened.

### A typical business-planning cycle

1. Review your current performance against last year or against your current year's targets.
2. Work out your opportunities and threats.
3. Analyse your successes and failures during the previous year.

4. Look at your key objectives for the coming year and move or re-establish your longer-term planning.

5. Identify and refine the resource implications of your review and draft a budget.

6. Define the new financial year's income statement and balance sheet targets.

7. Conclude the plan.

8. Review it regularly – for example, on a monthly basis – by monitoring performance, reviewing progress and achieving objectives.

9. Go back to 1.

## Budgets and budget planning

New small business owners may run their businesses in a relaxed way and may not see the need to budget. However, if you are planning for your business's future, you need to fund your plans. Budgeting is the most effective way to control your cash flow, allowing you to invest in new opportunities at the appropriate time.

If your business is growing, you may not always be able to be hands-on with every part of it. You may have to split your budget up into areas that are more manageable such as

*Draft your budget by splitting it up into manageable areas*

sales, production, marketing, etc. You will find that money starts to move in many different directions through your organisation, and budgets are a vital tool in ensuring that you stay solvent.

A budget is a plan to:

- control your finances
- enable you to make confident financial decisions and meet your objectives
- ensure you have enough money for your future projects.

It outlines what you will be spending your money on and how that spending will be financed. At the same time, a budget is not a forecast. A forecast is a prediction of the future whereas a budget is a planned outcome of the future – defined by your plan – that your business wants to achieve.

There are a number of benefits to drawing up a business budget, including a greater ability to:

- manage your money effectively
- allocate appropriate resources to projects
- monitor performance
- meet your objectives
- improve decision making
- identify problems before they occur – such as the need to raise finance or cash flow difficulties
- plan for the future
- increase staff motivation.

## Guidelines for drawing up a budget

There are a number of key factors you should consider to make sure your budgets and plans are as realistic and useful as possible.

### Make time for budgeting

It is worth setting aside some time to fully consider all the elements of your budget. If you invest time in creating a comprehensive and realistic budget, it will be easier to manage and ultimately be more effective.

### Use last year's figures – but only as a guide

Collect historical information on sales and costs if they are available. But also consider what your sales plans are, how your sales resources will be used and any changes in the competitive environment.

### Create realistic budgets

Use the historical information, your business plan and any changes in operations or priorities to budget for overheads and other fixed costs.

It is useful to work out the relationship between variable costs and sales and then use your sales forecast to project variable costs. For example, if your unit costs reduce by 10% for each additional 20%, how much will your unit costs decrease if you have a 33% rise in sales?

Make sure your budgets contain enough information for you to easily monitor the key drivers of your business such as sales, costs and working capital. Accounting software can help you manage your accounts.

### Involve the right people

If any of your staff have financial responsibilities – for example sales targets, production costs or specific projects – it is a good idea to get them involved at the planning stage so they understand the budget and feel comfortable working with it. Once they do, you can give them the responsibility for sticking to the budget.

Get your staff involved in setting sales and other targets.

## Checklist: what your budget should cover

First you need to decide how many budgets you really need. Many small businesses have one overall operating budget that sets out how much money is needed to run the business over the coming period – usually a year. As your business grows, your total operating budget is likely to be made up of several individual budgets, such as your marketing budget and your sales budgets.

However they are allocated, your budgets will need to include the following:

### Projected cash flow

Your cash flow budget projects your future cash position on a month-by-month basis. Budgeting in this way is vital for small businesses as it can pinpoint any difficulties you may encounter. It should be reviewed at least monthly.

### Costs

Typically, your business will have three kinds of costs:

- *fixed* costs are items such as rent, rates, salaries and financing costs

- *variable* costs include raw materials and overtime

- *one-off capital* costs, for example purchases of computer equipment or office furniture.

To forecast your costs you can either look at last year's records or contact your suppliers for quotes.

### Sales

Sales or revenue forecasts are typically based on a combination of your sales history and how effective you expect your future efforts to be.

Using your sales and expenditure forecasts, you can prepare projected profits for the next 12 months. In effect, what you will do is create an income statement, not of past sales and expenses, but of expected ones. This will enable you to analyse your margins and other key ratios such as your return on investment.

## Use your budget to measure performance

If you base your budget on your business plan, you will create a kind of financial action plan. This can serve several useful functions, particularly if you review your budgets regularly as part of your annual planning cycle.

Your budget can serve as:

- an indicator of the costs and revenues linked to each of your activities

- a way of providing information and supporting management decisions throughout the year

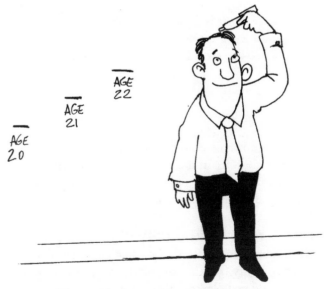

*Use your budget to measure performance*

- a means of monitoring and controlling your business, particularly if you analyse the differences between your actual and budgeted income.

### Benchmarking performance

Comparing your budget year on year can be an excellent way of benchmarking your business's performance – you can compare your projected figures, for example, with previous years to measure your performance.

You can also compare your figures for projected margins and growth with those of other companies, or across different parts of your business.

### Key performance indicators

To boost your business's performance you need to understand and monitor the key 'drivers' of your business. A driver is anything that has a major impact on your business. There are many factors affecting every business's performance, so it is vital to focus on a handful of these and monitor them carefully.

The three key areas for most businesses are:

- sales
- costs
- working capital.

Any trends towards cash flow problems or falling profit-ability will show up in these figures measured against your budgets and forecasts. They can help you spot problems early on if they are calculated on a consistent basis.

## Review your budget regularly

To use your budgets effectively, you must review and revise them frequently. This is particularly true if your business is growing and you plan to move into new areas.

Using up-to-date budgets enables you to be flexible, and lets you manage your cash flow and identify what needs to be achieved in the next budgeting period.

The three main areas to consider are:

### Your actual income

Each month, compare your actual income with your sales budget by:

- analysing the reasons for any shortfall, for example lower sales volumes, flat markets or under-performing products

- analysing the reasons for a particularly high turnover, for example whether your targets were too low

- comparing the timing of your income with your projections and checking that they fit.

Analysing these variations will help you to set future budgets and also allow you to take action where needed.

### Your actual expenditure

Regularly review your actual expenditure against your budget. This will help you to predict future costs with better reliability. You should:

- look at how your fixed costs differed from your budget

- check that your variable costs were in line with your budget – usually, variable costs adjust in line with your sales volume

- analyse any reasons for changes in the relationship between costs and turnover

- analyse any differences in the timing of your expenditure, for example by checking suppliers' payment terms.

*Make sure your budget suits your circumstances*

### Breakeven

You need to calculate the breakeven point in your company regularly. Breakeven is the point at which your gross margin covers your fixed overheads. Breakeven can be calculated either in terms of units of production or in rands. It is a very useful calculation: After you have reached breakeven point, you know you have covered costs and will now start making a profit.

# FIFTEEN KEY BUSINESS CALCULATIONS

*Lesley-Caren Johnson*

## INTRODUCTION

So many business people feel that they do not have the knowledge necessary to manage and monitor the financial health of their businesses. They hand over this responsibility to a financial manager, accountant or auditor. Don't do this! To manage and grow your business effectively, you must understand your financial statements. You can then take corrective action or make decisions based on this information. If you use the services of a bookkeeper or accountant, stipulate how you would like the management reports presented to you, how often you want them and what additional information you require.

Your objective as a manager or business owner should be to:

- provide reliable and useful financial information pertaining to the business's financial performance and overall health

- safeguard the business assets and records.

If you can read and understand the financial statements in your business, you can do the financial calculations discussed in this chapter. This will ensure that you are always in control of the financial performance of the operation.

## THE IMPORTANCE OF PERFORMING PERIODIC BUSINESS CALCULATIONS

It is important to review your financial statements on a regular basis – the income statement every month and the balance sheet at least twice a year or more often if you make major changes in the business. However, unless you convert the information presented in the financial statements to a format where it can be accurately compared, you are not going to benefit from it. For example, you can review the income statement at the end of every month and note that the gross profit is greater than the expenses and therefore the business shows a net profit, but are you able to determine whether the gross profit is acceptable and in line with your budgets or other businesses in your industry? The answer is no!

Isolated figures tell you nothing and can be very misleading. What you really need to do is convert all figures into a format in which they can be used to compare this year's figures with others from:

- the same/current year

- previous years (history)

- competitors or industry norms

- planned (budgeted) figures.

By reviewing your financial statements periodically and performing the financial calculations, you will be in a better position to take corrective action if your performance does not measure up to your projections (budgets) and also to plan for the future more accurately. The business calculations discussed in this chapter have been divided into two main sections: operational calculations and financial calculations. These calculations will help you measure the following areas and resources invested in the business:

- Profitability of the business based on monitoring gross profit and business expenses

- Breakeven point and safety margin for the business

- The relationship between gross margin and mark-up and the effect of discounting

- The solvency of the business and where the money invested in the business is used

- How efficiently the money invested is used

- How efficiently the stock is managed

- The financial return achieved on the money invested in the business

- How well you manage your debtors and creditors books

- How much free cash flow exists in the business.

## REASONS WHY BUSINESSES FAIL

There are many reasons why businesses fail. One of the most common reasons is that business owners do not keep their fingers on the pulse of the business and do not analyse the financial and operational performance of the business regularly enough. Other business owners may only review the profitability of the business, and so long as the business shows a net profit every month they are satisfied that the organisation is financially sound.

*Sink or swim! Do you understand your company's financial statements?*

Remember that profit is only an estimate of the business's sales less the expenses, and is affected by issues such as stock levels and depreciation. Problem areas can be highlighted quickly and corrective action taken timeously if you review your financial statements regularly and interpret them correctly. The following are some of the reasons why businesses fail and the issues that can contribute to failure. We have also provided you with guidelines as to which calculation(s) you should be performing if you identify one or more of the issues as potential weak spots in your business.

## Shortage of cash

### *Factors that may contribute to the issue*

- The owners take too much of the profits out of the business. Some profit should be retained in the business and carried forward to the new year to be used for working capital or upgrades, etc.

- Rapid expansion strategies are implemented. In order to cope with the expected growth, too much extra stock is purchased and the working capital is not sufficient to cope with the burden.

- The value of fixed assets is far greater than the value of current assets and they cannot be converted quickly enough to cash if needed.

- Poor cash flow planning and failure to take extraordinary events into account.

- A major debtor may default on payment, which could place you in an adverse cash flow position where you are unable to pay your creditors.

- Unexpected cash demands, for example a sudden increase in expenses, interest rates, creditor price increases, etc.

- Unexpected drop in sales.

- Large stockholding or stock you cannot sell.

- Fraud or theft committed in the business, especially by staff who have access to stock and money.

### Possible calculations
- Current ratio and quick ratio
- Debtors trading cycle and payment period
- Creditors trading cycle and payment period
- Stock turnover rate

## Insufficient profitability
### Factors that may contribute to the issue
- Poor profit margins as a result of lack of control over cost of sales and expenses.

- Staff costs are generally one of the highest business operating expenses. It is too easy to keep staff on in positions where you do not need them or where they are not productive.

- Fierce or lack of competition can contribute to poor profitability. Fierce competition may mean too many of the same products or services on the market and can lead to price wars, whereas too little competition can affect the supply and demand of the product.

- You may sometimes purchase products from new suppliers. A number of problems may arise, such as cheaper prices at the start of the relationship with sudden high increases in the short-term, inferior products and unreliable supply of products. All these problems can impact on customer service and therefore turnover, which will affect profitability in the long term.

- Product life cycles and reduced demand, especially for seasonal goods. It is not a good idea to focus your whole business on a range of products that are winners in the winter months but where there is no demand for them in the summer months.

- High overheads – watch those expenses (see the benchmarks in Appendix 4).

- Failure to reinvest in new equipment means that not only will old equipment cost you more in maintenance and repairs but you may find you are unable to produce the goods due to equipment failure. Plan ahead and make allowances for the purchase of new equipment.

- Lack of research and development – know your market and trends, and provide goods and/or services that meet customer needs.

- Business owners are often offered discounted pricing by suppliers if they purchase in bulk. Be careful of this as sometime suppliers are trying to offload merchandise before a sell-by date or before a new model is introduced. You do not want to sit with outdated or useless stock you cannot sell.

- Ensure that you decide on effective marketing campaigns and identify advertising mediums that work for you in order to move stock quickly.

- If you are in an industry that is seasonal or where technology is fast-changing, make sure that you allow for changes in technology, fashion or trends so that you are not left with outdated stock.

- Some businesses rely heavily on a few key customers. This can be dangerous as losing just one of those customers can have a detrimental effect on the business and can severely limit the growth of the business.

**Possible calculations**
- Cost of sales percentage
- Gross profit margin
- Expense ratios
- Staff productivity ratios
- Stock turnover rate

## Poor management
### Factors that may contribute to the issue

- Recruiting the wrong staff for your type of operation.
- Not performing the necessary induction and staff training so that staff can perform their duties adequately.

- Lack of motivation and discipline leads to staff problems in a business, such as low productivity, theft, and poor attendance and time-keeping.

- Poor communication with staff has a negative effect on the business as it affects staff motivation, customer service, etc.

- Employee relations and staff turnover rates – employing new staff and training them to a point where they can perform their functions efficiently takes time and money.

- Public relations and general reputation of the business.

- Monitor your recruitment and selection methods and ensure that staff are trained and adequately communicated with.

### Possible calculations

- Staff productivity ratio
- Staff costs (expense) as a percentage of sales

## WHICH FINANCIAL STATEMENTS WILL YOU NEED?

The figures you need to do the business calculations are found on the income statement and the balance sheet.

The *income statement* deals with the operational or trading activities and thus shows you the results of these trading activities over a specific period of time. You should draw up an income statement at the end of every month but you can draw it up more often, such as weekly, if you wish.

The *balance sheet* deals with the money invested in the business and shows the business's financial position at a specific point in time. The balance sheet is generally prepared twice a year – at the end of the first six months and then again at financial year-end. It may be prepared more often if major changes take place in the business and you wish to review the allocation of the resources in the business.

**Note:** You may have heard the saying 'garbage in, garbage out' – this is very true of financial information. If errors were made when the figures were entered into the financial statements, then the calculations you perform will also result in false information. Figures must be checked for accuracy.

Examples of an income statement and balance sheet have been included. The figures we use later will be taken from these examples. Please note that the financial statements represent a *financial period* of six months. When we compare turnover figures, for example, we will do so for the first six months of 2003 with the same period for 2002.

*Garbage in, garbage out*

*Finance in your own business*

**Income statement for the six months ended 30 June 2011**

| | | 6 months ended 30 June 2011 | 6 months ended 30 June 2010 |
|---|---|---|---|
| 1 | **Sales** | **1 745 400** | **1 538 710** |
| 2 | **Cost of sales** | **1 126 420** | **1 015 340** |
| 3 | Opening stock | 338 370 | 312 390 |
| 4 | Purchases | 1 148 890 | 1 041 320 |
| 5 | Closing stock | 360 840 | 338 370 |
| 6 | **Gross profit** | **618 980** | **523 370** |
| 7 | Other operating income | 68 800 | 76 240 |
| | | 687 780 | 599 610 |
| 8 | **Expenses** | **540 694** | **473 990** |
| 9 | Accounting & auditing | 7 200 | 6 450 |
| 10 | Advertising & marketing | 10 090 | 9 050 |
| 11 | Motor vehicle expenses | 18 500 | 16 650 |
| 12 | Rent | 157 086 | 144 450 |
| 13 | Stationery | 3 000 | 2 750 |
| 14 | Repairs & maintenance | 4 800 | 4 400 |
| 15 | Telephone | 8 250 | 7 425 |
| 16 | Water & electricity | 9 000 | 8 100 |
| 17 | Interest on loan | 24 800 | 19 110 |
| 18 | Salaries & wages | 296 718 | 254 500 |
| 19 | Packaging | 1 250 | 1 105 |
| 20 | **Net profit (before tax & depreciation)** | **147 086** | **125 620** |

**Note:** Net profit is also referred to as the bottom line. The income statement must reflect what other business expenses have been excluded from the net profit. These expenses may include interest on loans, tax, depreciation and dividends.

**Balance sheet as at 30 June 2011**

|  |  | 30 June 2011 | 30 June 2010 |
|---|---|---|---|
| 21 | **ASSETS** | | |
| 22 | **Fixed assets** | **832 490** | **733 760** |
| 23 | Property, plant & equipment | 498 040 | 362 930 |
| 24 | Intangible assets | 133 230 | 117 150 |
| 25 | Investments | 26 430 | 7 820 |
| 26 | Other invesments & non-current rec | 105 880 | 245 860 |
| 27 | Deferred tax | 68 910 | 0 |
| 28 | **Current assets** | **845 500** | **829 300** |
| 29 | Stock | 360 840 | 338 370 |
| 30 | Debtors | 445 320 | 490 770 |
| 31 | SARS | 160 | 160 |
| 32 | Cash & cash equivalents | 39 180 | 0 |
| 33 | **Total assets** | **1 677 990** | **1 563 060** |
| 34 | **EQUITY & LIABILITIES** | | |
| 35 | **Capital & reserves** | **795 860** | **768 070** |
| 36 | Long-term loan | 188 050 | 137 420 |
| 37 | **Current liabilities** | **694 080** | **657 570** |
| 38 | Creditors | 685 720 | 618 950 |
| 39 | SARS | 8 360 | 0 |
| 40 | Bank overdraft | 0 | 38 620 |
| 41 | **Total equity & liabilities** | **1 677 990** | **1 563 060** |

**Note:** Reserves are unused profits that are carried over to the balance sheet and included as equity. In this example, Capital = Owners equity or Investment and Reserves = Retained profit

Debtors (No. 30) can also be Accounts receivable
SARS (No. 31) can be shown as Current tax receivable
Creditors (No. 38) can also be Accounts payable
SARS (No. 39) can be shown as Current tax payable

## THE FIFTEEN CRITICAL BUSINESS CALCULATIONS

We have selected the fifteen calculations we feel will provide you with the most valuable information. For each calculation we provide a definition of the concept, explain why it is important that you perform the function, give you the formula for the calculation and then tell you how to use the information you have in order to analyse your financial results. All figures used in the calculations have been extracted from the examples of the financial statements provided on pages 126 and 127.

### Operational calculations

The figures you require in order to calculate the operational efficiency of the business are all taken from the income statement. Because this report is produced on a monthly

*Measure your operational efficiency monthly*

basis, all the calculations discussed here can be performed monthly too. This means that when the results do not measure up either to your budgets or to industry norms and benchmarks, you can take corrective action immediately.

## Gross profit

The *gross profit* is the amount of money you have left over after you have paid your suppliers for the stock you purchased for resale purposes. To calculate the gross profit you must first work out your *cost of sales* and then subtract this figure from your turnover.

*Cost of sales* is the amount of money it cost you to achieve your sales and is thus the amount you pay your suppliers for these products when you purchased them. However, in order to determine an accurate cost of sales you must take your stockholding at specific times into account.

**Note:** Many businesses do not sell a product but rather provide a service so there is no stock in service-type businesses. However, there may be other business expenses that the owner sees as a direct cost necessary to provide that service to the customer. These costs could include people such as sales representatives or even the cost of consultants doing the work. The cost of this resource could be seen as a cost of sales as opposed to an operational cost. In a manufacturing concern, the cost of product (raw materials) as well as labour used to produce a finished product may all form part of the cost of sales.

Calculating the cost of sales and gross profit allows you to monitor your sales and the stock in the business and compare the figures to the previous month or the same period the previous year. But doing it this way means that you are comparing isolated figures and you know that this can be misleading. You must therefore convert the actual figures to percentages. When you calculate the gross profit as a percentage of the turnover, the result is the *gross profit margin (%)*. This makes it easier to compare the results and manage the performance. You must know the following formulas in order to analyse the gross profit information.

Cost of sales = Opening stock + Purchases – Closing stock

| **Opening stock** | The value of the stock on hand at the beginning of the period and determined from a full stock count. |
| Plus: **Purchases** | The value of all stock purchased during the period that you sold to customers. |
| Less: **Closing stock** | The value of the stock on hand at the end of the period and determined from a full stock count. |

Gross profit = Sales – Cost of sales

The sales figure shown on the income statement represents the net sales generated from the business's main trading activities, excluding VAT.

Making a profit is the main objective of every business, and profitability ratios measure whether or not you have achieved this objective. Calculating the gross profit margin provides you with an indication of the effectiveness of the business's pricing policy and how well purchases and production were controlled.

$$\text{Gross profit margin} = \frac{\text{Gross profit}}{\text{Sales}} \times 100$$

---

**Practical example**

Extract the following information from the income and expense statement for the 2011 period:

Sales (1)          = R1 745 400

---

Opening stock (3)   = R338 370

Purchases (4)       = R1 148 890

Closing stock (5)   = R360 840

Cost of sales   = Opening stock (3) + Purchases (4) − Closing stock (5)

                = 338 370 + 1 148 890 − 360 840

                = 1 126 420

Gross profit (6) = Sales (1) − Cost of sales (2)

                = 1 745 400 − 1 126 420

                = 618 980

Gross profit margin (%)  $= \dfrac{\text{Gross profit (6)}}{\text{Sales (1)}} \times 100$

$= \dfrac{618\,980}{1\,745\,400} \times 100$

$= 35{,}46\%$

If you perform the same calculations for the 2010 period and convert the gross profit to a percentage as we did in the example, the result is 34,01%. You can now compare the two periods and determine whether or not your current year's gross profit margin is in line with the previous year. As can be seen from the example, the gross profit for 2011 improved by almost 1,5% over what was achieved in 2010. Use this information as follows:

- Generally, each industry has a gross profit margin average. Compare your gross profit margin to the industry norm or benchmark. You should aim to meet or exceed this benchmark in your business.

- Compare your gross profit margin to your budgeted figure. Did you achieve the desired percentage? If your margin is higher than your budgeted figure, then you must review the financial statements and determine a reason for the increased margin.

- When you set budgets for a new year, you will generally use the figures from the previous year as your base. You must determine whether these figures are accurate in terms of industry norms and your operation specifically. If you feel that your gross profit margin was too low in the previous year, then you will budget to improve on that figure for the new year, but you must put steps in place for how you plan to achieve this goal.

- Because you are using stock value and sales figures to calculate the gross profit (and gross profit margin), it stands to reason that if the outcome achieved is not the desired one, then you must review relevant activities. For example, were all sales put through the business? Did you count your stock correctly? Are you calculating the value of stock on hand using the correct cost prices, i.e. what you paid for the goods. Is your pricing structure correct? Remember that calculating this figure gives you an indication of what is happening with the stock in the business and could point to a shrinkage problem. Shrinkage is theft or wastage. If your gross profit margin is too low (because your cost of sales is too high), then you can put systems in place to monitor stock more closely and try to reduce the shrinkage.

It is of little use to compile an income statement once a year and to then be dissatisfied when you calculate the gross profit margin and find you have not met your budgets. The income statement should be compiled monthly and the gross profit margin calculated immediately to ensure that if there is a problem relating to turnover levels or stock management, you can immediately take steps to correct the situation and prevent the same problems arising in the next month.

## The breakeven point and safety margin

The *breakeven point* in a business reflects the amount of sales or income required to ensure sufficient gross profit to pay all operating expenses where the business makes a zero net profit, that is, neither a profit nor a loss. The *safety margin* shows the amount of sales that can be lost before the business begins trading below the breakeven point and therefore at a loss.

Knowing your breakeven point and safety margin ensures that you are aware of how many sales you must do every month just to ensure you have sufficient money to pay your expenses. Once you have achieved the breakeven point during the month, you know the business is then beginning to operate profitably.

$$\text{Breakeven point} = \frac{\text{Expenses}}{\text{Gross profit margin}}$$

$$\text{Safety margin} = \frac{\text{Actual sales} - \text{Breakeven sales}}{\text{Actual sales}} \times 100$$

---

**Practical example**

Extract the following information from the income and expense statement for the 2011 period:

Expenses (8)  = R540 694

Sales (1)    = R1 745 400

We have already calculated the gross profit margin so we know this is 35,46%. Therefore our calculation is as follows:

$$\text{Breakeven point} = \frac{\text{Expenses (8)}}{\text{Gross profit margin}}$$

$$= \frac{540\ 694}{35,46\%}$$

$$= \text{R1 524 799}$$

---

This means that the business must bring in R1 524 799 in sales to pay all the expenses as well as cover the cost of sales. In other words, the business will break even when it makes exactly R1 524 799 in sales.

$$\text{Safety margin} = \frac{\text{Actual sales (1)} - \text{Breakeven sales}}{\text{Actual sales (1)}} \times 100$$

$$= \frac{1\,745\,400 - 1\,524\,799}{1\,745\,400} \times 100$$

$$= 12{,}64\%$$

This means that the business can only afford to lose 12,64% or R220 618 of its actual sales before it begins to operate at a loss.

You should have a clear understanding of your average breakeven point. If your expenses are fixed, then you can calculate breakeven and be reasonably sure that the average breakeven will hold true for most of the financial year. If, however, you are in a business where your expenses fluctuate quite substantially, then you should calculate your breakeven point on a monthly basis to be sure that you are generating sufficient income to pay all operating costs. Once you know what your business's breakeven point is, you can then use this information to adjust your expenses or sales figures and determine the effect this will have on your breakeven turnover.

We know that at the current sales and expenses this business needs to generate R1 524 799 in sales to break even, but what would happen if:

a) the expenses increased to R601 500 or

b) the gross margin decreased to 34%?

What effect would this have on the breakeven point? Let's take a look.

a) Breakeven point $= \dfrac{\text{Expenses}}{\text{Gross profit margin}}$

$= \dfrac{601\ 500}{35,46\%}$

$= \text{R1}\ 696\ 277$

*Know your breakeven point or risk going down*

The expenses increased and therefore the breakeven point is higher.

b) Breakeven point = $\dfrac{\text{Expenses}}{\text{Gross profit margin}}$

$= \dfrac{540\ 694}{34\%}$

= R1 590 276

The gross profit margin is lower, which means the cost of sales is higher and therefore the breakeven point is higher.

## Mark-up

*Mark-up* is the difference between the selling price and the cost price of a product. We mark up products from cost price (the price we pay the supplier for the item) to selling price to achieve a specific gross profit margin. Therefore a direct relationship exists between mark-up and the gross profit margin.

Use the mark-up formula to calculate the average mark-up percentage based on the gross profit margin. When you have established the average mark-up percentage, you can apply it to any new products you purchase for resale.

Average mark-up = $\dfrac{\text{Gross profit}}{\text{Cost of sales}} \times 100$

---

**Practical example**

Extract the following information from the income and expense statement for the 2011 period:

Gross profit (6) = R618 980

Cost of sales (2) = R1 126 420

Mark-up $= \dfrac{\text{Gross profit (6)}}{\text{Gross of sales (2)}} \times 100$

$= \dfrac{618\ 980}{1\ 126\ 420} \times 100$

= 54,95%

---

This means that on average we are marking up the cost price of the goods we sell by 54,95%.

Now that we know our average mark-up, we can calculate the selling price of new products by adding a mark-up of 54,95% to the cost price. This will ensure that we still achieve our gross profit margin of 35,46%.

If we purchased an item from our supplier for R12,50 and marked the item up by 54,95%, the selling price would be R19,37. If we then calculated the gross profit margin on the item, the result would be:

$$\frac{(19,37 - 12,50)}{19,37} \times 100 = 35,46\%$$

If you calculate the average mark-up for the 2010 period, the figure is 51,55%. Thus our average mark-up in the previous year was lower than in the current year. This may account for the increase in the gross profit margin between 2010 (34,01%) and 2011 (35,46%).

You can also use the mark-up/margin calculations to determine your proposed selling price and then decide if the market can handle that price. You may decide in some instances that the selling price is too high as your customers will not pay that price. You will therefore have to reduce the mark-up, thereby effectively reducing your gross profit margin as well. In other instances you may find that your calculated selling price is low compared to your competitors. You may then decide to increase the mark-up and therefore increase the gross profit margin.

When calculating mark-up, all cost price figures must exclude VAT. The selling price you calculate will then also exclude VAT. In the example, we calculated that an item with a cost price of R12,50 was marked up by 54,95% to a selling price of R19,37. This selling price is VAT exclusive, so to determine the actual price the customer will pay for the item we must add VAT as follows:

$$R19{,}37 \times \frac{14 \text{ (VAT is 14\%)}}{100}$$
$$= R2{,}71$$

Therefore R2,71 plus R19,37 is equal to a VAT inclusive selling price of R22,08 for this item.

## Benchmarking expenses

The term 'benchmarking' refers to standardised figures in the form of a percentage that are used to monitor some or all of our business expenses from one period to the next. Some business expenses are fixed, such as rent, salaries, interest on motor vehicles or loan repayments and accounting fees. Other expenses such as telephone, wages and motor vehicle expenses vary every month. In order to determine whether the fixed and variable expenses are in line with budgets and industry norms you must convert them to percentages. You can do this in one of two ways:

- You can calculate the expense as a percentage of your turnover.

- You can calculate the expense as a percentage of your gross profit.

**Note:** Remember that you must be consistent, so do not calculate expenses as a percentage of turnover one month, and the next month as a percentage of gross profit. Decide which formula you are going to use and stick to it.

The formula to convert expenses to a percentage is either:

$$\frac{\text{Expense}}{\text{Sales}} \times 100 \text{ or } \frac{\text{Expense}}{\text{Gross profit}} \times 100$$

**Practical example**

For the purposes of this exercise we have calculated the expense item as a percentage of sales. The information you need to convert your expenses to percentages are the sales figures for 2010 and 2011 and the actual amounts of the Motor vehicle (11), Rent (12), Telephone (15) and Salaries (18) expenses for both years. Extract this information from the income statement.

| Expense item | Calculation 2010 | Calculation 2011 |
|---|---|---|
| Motor vehicle (11) | $\frac{16\,650}{1\,538\,710} \times 100$<br><br>$= 1{,}08\%$ | $\frac{18\,500}{1\,745\,400} \times 100$<br><br>$= 1{,}06\%$ |
| Rent (12) | $\frac{144\,450}{1\,538\,710} \times 100$<br><br>$= 9{,}38\%$ | $\frac{157\,086}{1\,745\,400} \times 100$<br><br>$= 9\%$ |
| Telephone (15) | $\frac{7\,425}{1\,538\,710} \times 100$<br><br>$= 0{,}48\%$ | $\frac{8\,250}{1\,745\,400} \times 100$<br><br>$= 0{,}47\%$ |
| Salaries (18) | $\frac{254\,500}{1\,538\,710} \times 100$<br><br>$= 16{,}54\%$ | $\frac{296\,718}{1\,745\,400} \times 100$<br><br>$= 17\%$ |

What does this mean? Let's look at each expense item separately.

### Motor vehicle expenses

This expense item remained much the same over the two financial periods. If motor vehicle expenses are directly related to sales, for example, sales reps using company resources to visit clients, then this figure may be higher than shown in the example as they may spend more money getting to clients. What you must consider, though, is that if you noticed an increase in this expense because you employed more sales staff, then you must ensure that the extra expense was warranted. Income or sales must have increased as a direct result of having these sales people on the road marketing to your customers and generally selling more. In the previous example, our motor vehicle expenses stayed the same but our turnover increased by 13%. Was this because the sales reps worked harder, or did you increase the selling price of your goods by 13%?

If, on the other hand, your business does not rely on sales staff using company vehicles and you saw a sharp increase in these expenses, look at where the money was spent. It may have been on excessive vehicle repairs or increased fuel bills. You must then review what the vehicle is costing you to maintain and consider replacing it or putting some controls in place to limit the amount of fuel your employees are using on your account.

*Monitor all business expenses*

### Rent

The rental on the business's premises increased by 8,75% from 2010 to 2011. This was probably an annual increase, yet when we calculate rental as a percentage of turnover, we are spending slightly less in the current year as the percentage has decreased from 9,38% to 9%. Rent can be either a fixed expense, such as when you pay a set amount each month, or it can be a variable expense. Rent is a variable expense if your lease agreement includes a turnover clause so that you pay a percentage of your turnover as rent each month.

### Telephone

Telephone expenses remained the same over the two periods when converted from an actual figure to a percentage, even though we spent more in rand terms in the current year as opposed to the previous year. If your business relies on telesales marketing then the actual increase can be attributed to sales staff making more telesales calls. If not, then you may have to review your telephone accounts and find out why this expense is higher in actual terms. Your employees could be taking advantage of the telephones and using this business tool for their private use. This is an expense that can become excessive if not properly controlled. Review your telephone expenditure every month.

### Salaries

Even though the figures show only a slight increase in this expense from 2010 to 2011, if you calculate the actual increase year on year you will note that salaries increased by 16,58% while the turnover only increased by just over 13%. The reason for this may be that you gave your employees salary increases in 2011 or it could also mean that you employed additional staff in a telesales call centre or as sales reps to assist with marketing. Some businesses, especially retail and food operations, generally have to employ more staff during peak seasons and holidays to cope with the additional customer demand. You will therefore see an increase in salaries and wages over these periods. Remember that if you do not achieve sales budgets during these periods but have employed extra staff, you must cut back on the extra staff so that your salaries and wages expense is still in line with your average benchmark.

We have provided several examples of business expenses that you can convert to percentages in order to monitor these each month of the year. You may decide to convert all your expenses to percentages each month, or you may decide to only convert the ones you think are problematic in your business.

## Ratio analysis

Before we start calculating ratios, let's look at some important points in this regard:

- When calculating ratios it is important that data or financial figures for the same period are used.

- Remember that when extracting information from a balance sheet, you must calculate an average by taking the previous year plus the current year and dividing by two to get a realistic figure.

- If only the current year's information is taken from the balance sheet, the result will be a distorted ratio. For example, the company only implemented a credit facility for customers during the last quarter of the financial year, or half the company's assets were sold after the first six months of the financial period. An income statement figure is for a whole period, for example a year, and therefore the current year's information is sufficient – we do not have to use an average. This is the formula to calculate the average:

$$\text{Average} = \frac{\text{Previous period value} + \text{Current period value}}{2}$$

**Note:** Ratios tell us how one number is related to another number. We use ratios to make comparisons between two things. When we express ratios in words, we use the word 'to' – we say 'the ratio of something to something else'.

## Staff productivity ratio

Salaries and wages and all costs associated with your employees generally amount to a large portion of the total expenses of the business. You must ensure that the staff you employ are productive and effective in assisting you to grow your business. In order to monitor staff performance, calculate their productivity using the following formula expressed as a ratio. Staff costs are the total cost to the company of your employees and include salaries and wages, PAYE, Unemployment Insurance Fund (UIF), skills levy, pension or provident fund contributions as well as medical aid contributions, etc.

$$\text{Staff productivity ratio} = \frac{\text{Sales}}{\text{Staff costs}}$$

---

**Practical example**

Extract the following information from the income statement (we have used the 2011 financial year's figures):

Sales (1)                           = R1 745 400

Staff costs (Salaries) (18)  = R296 718

Staff productivity ratio      $= \dfrac{\text{Sales (1)}}{\text{Staff costs (18)}}$

$= \dfrac{1\ 745\ 400}{296\ 718} = 5{,}88{:}1$

This means that for every R1 I spend on my staff, I make R5,88 in turnover or sales.

---

*Finance in your own business*

In the example we ask what the ratio of staff costs to sales is and our answer is R1 (staff costs) to R5,88 (sales). You can monitor your staff productivity ratio monthly or do it several times during the year, perhaps quarterly to ensure that you are always getting maximum performance from your employees. If this ratio dropped, say to 3,5:1, you will then have to determine the cause of the drop, for example seasonal changes, staff non-performance or too many staff, and take the necessary corrective action. The areas of the business that may impact on this ratio are:

- Sales
  - If sales decrease, the ratio will drop: less customers = less sales = less for staff to do.

*Using the staff productivity ratio could be an eye-opener*

- If sales increase, the ratio will improve: more customers = more income or sales = busier and more productive staff.

■ Staff costs

- If this expense increases but sales stay the same, then the ratio will drop: more staff to do the same amount of work = less productive employees as they will be spreading the workload amongst more of them.

- If this expense is controlled and reduced, the ratio will improve: less staff to do the same amount of work = more productive employees.

## Net profit margin and ratio

The aim of any business is to make a profit. We do not just want to look at the bottom line or net profit and see that we made a profit or a loss, we also want to calculate that profit:

■ as a percentage of our turnover

■ as a ratio to turnover.

The *net profit ratio* tells us the amount of net profit per R1 of turnover a business has earned. After taking into account the cost of sales, the administration costs, the selling and distribution costs and all other operational costs (expenses), the net profit is the profit that is left, out of which a business will pay interest, tax, dividends, etc.

Let's take a look at the formulas for calculating the net profit margin and the net profit ratio.

$$\text{Net profit margin} = \frac{\text{Net profit}}{\text{Sales}} \times 100$$

$$\text{Net profit ratio} = \frac{\text{Sales}}{\text{Net profit}}$$

---

**Practical example**

Extract the following information from the income statement for the 2010 and 2011 periods:

|  | | 2010 | 2011 |
|---|---|---|---|
| Sales (1) | = | R1 538 710 | R1 745 400 |
| Net profit (before tax) (20) | = | R125 620 | R147 086 |

$$\text{Net profit margin} = \frac{125\,620}{1\,538\,710} \times 100 \quad \frac{147\,086}{1\,745\,400} \times 100$$

$$= 8,16\% \qquad 8,43\%$$

$$\text{Net profit ratio} = \frac{1\,538\,710}{125\,620} \quad \frac{1\,745\,400}{147\,086}$$

$$= 12,25:1 \qquad 11,87:1$$

The net profit margin is the net profit before (or after) tax, dividends, depreciation, etc. expressed as a percentage of the sales. The net profit ratio tells us that for every R12,25 (2010) or R11,87 (2011) worth of sales, we make R1 of net profit.

---

Our net profit increased by 17,09% from 2010 to 2011 compared to the increase in sales of only 13,4%. This shows that we managed the business income and expenses effectively over the course of the year and in fact were more profitable in the second year. The net profit ratio to sales or turnover, however, is lower in 2011. The reason why the net profit ratio has decreased while the net profit percentage has increased is because higher net profits will give fewer coverage on sales. The higher the net profit, the lower the ratio, and vice versa. The lower the net profit, the more funds are required to cover sales, and therefore the ratio will be high.

## Cash flow

*Cash flow* is the movement of money into and out of a business, which results from payments to the company (sales, debtors) and payments by it (suppliers, expenses). The first step towards creating positive cash flow is that the business must generate net profit and must be able to pay its long-term loans and capital expenses out of the net profit. Over a period of time this will lead to a build-up of *working capital*, which can then be used to enhance and improve the business.

A negative cash flow occurs when you do not have enough cash to fund your business. For example:

- your expenses exceed your gross profit rand value

- you exceed your purchase budget

- you pay your creditors too soon

- your debtors pay you late.

New businesses must be especially careful to combat negative cash flow. Negative cash flow or cash flow problems often occur within the first year of trading. Remember the following:

- Do not be tempted to overspend during this period.

- Be aware of debtors and debtors growth.

- Control stock levels.

- Set up credit terms with your suppliers.

Cash flow forecasting is an educated estimate of what money will flow into the business and how much will flow out during a particular period in the near future. Create this document on a monthly basis, and always prepare three months in advance. By comparing estimates with actual figures at the end of each month, you will soon develop a very accurate system of forecasting. The advantages of forecasting your cash flow and monitoring it on a periodic basis are the following:

- You are better able to control creditors.

- You are better able to plan expenditure.

- You are better able to control any overdraft.

- You can use less money to fund the business.

It is important to forecast cash flow, as sometimes unexpected events occur that can seriously affect your business and for which you did not budget. By doing a cash flow forecast you can make provision for unexpected costs. A cash flow forecast will also determine your money needs in the future. Your bank manager will be far more willing to assist you with an overdraft if you can clearly lay out your needs. When preparing your cash flow forecast, you must take all income and expense channels into account. Look at the following lists as they will give you a good idea of what information you need.

- **Cash flowing in:** opening bank balance; cash receipts from sales and debtors; income from the sale of an asset; interest received

- **Cash flowing out:** product purchases from suppliers; accounting; advertising; bank charges; cleaning; equipment leases; insurance; interest paid; rent; repairs and maintenance; salaries; stationery; telephone; transport; uniforms; vehicle; VAT; wages and casual wages; capital expenditure such as loan repayments or equipment purchases

Sales and income from debtors or any other source are shown in the cash flow forecast as total sales. These amounts include VAT. It is the actual amount received. The same applies to all money going out of the business – show all expense forecasts as VAT inclusive. You can see from the list that we also forecast for VAT as it is money flowing out of the business.

**Remember:** Capital expenditure items such as a loan repayment or new equipment purchases are not expenses that are included on the income statement, but they must be paid for out of available cash resources and are therefore included in the cash flow forecast. Total cash expenditure must be subtracted from total projected income and the result is how much cash you have available in the business or what your cash shortfall is for the period.

## Financial calculations

Most of the figures you require to perform the financial calculations are taken from your balance sheet. You will generally only produce a balance sheet once or twice a year, but these calculations should be performed as often as the operational calculations as the information gained is invaluable to the long-term management and decision-making processes in the business.

## Working capital

*Working capital* is the difference between the value of *current assets* and *current liabilities*. It is important to know how much working capital you have in the business as it tells you how much surplus liquid funds you have. It does not matter how profitable a business is; if it does not have adequate liquid resources it could become *insolvent*. This means that the business does not have sufficient cash resources to meet its immediate liabilities. This is one of the most vital aspects of finance. Many profitable companies have gone bust because they have missed the importance of their cash flow and liquidity. Remember that in the short term, cash flow and liquidity are far more important than profitability.

Working capital is what is left over after you cover all your current liabilities. Working capital is normally expressed in terms of current assets. *Current assets* are assets that are easily converted into cash during the normal course of business. Thus current assets include:

- stock (and raw materials)
- work in progress
- debts for collection, such as accounts receivable or short-term loans you have extended to an employee or a director
- cash.

The liquidity of current assets varies from asset to asset. Cash is the most liquid of your assets because it is already cash. Work in progress and accounts receivable (debtors) are the next most liquid assets since they are only steps away from completion and thus becoming cash. If you purchase stock to resell in the same form, then after cash, stock will be your next most liquid asset as you only need to sell an item to convert it to cash.

*Current liabilities* are debts that are repayable in a short period of time during the normal course of business. Thus current liabilities include the money you owe your

*Check the liquidity of your business monthly*

suppliers and other creditors, bills payable, bank overdraft and accrued tax.

Working capital = Current assets − Current liabilities

---

**Practical example**

Extract the following information from the balance sheet for the 2010 and 2011 financial years:

|  | 2010 | 2011 |
|---|---|---|
| Current assets (28) | 829 300 | 845 500 |
| Current liabilities (37) | 657 570 | 694 080 |
| Working capital | 829 300 | 845 500 |
|  | − 657 570 | − 694 080 |
|  | 171 730 | 151 420 |

---

It is vital that a business ensures it has sufficient liquid resources to cover its immediate liabilities. Look at it this way: If you review the debtors and creditors values on the balance sheet you will see that our debtors owe us R445 320 whereas we owe our creditors R685 720. First of all, our current liability (creditor) is greater than the current asset (debtor) and we have to rely on our debtors to pay us timeously. Secondly, it only takes one of these creditors to demand immediate payment and we could find ourselves in trouble if we did not have sufficient cash available to make the payment. Calculate your working capital figure every month.

## Working capital ratios

These ratios are also known as liquidity ratios and indicate the business's ability to meet its obligations. Liquid assets are assets that can easily be turned into cash. Working capital needs to be controlled as it is the total amount

of money that is in daily use in the business. In order
to calculate how effectively we control and manage our
working capital and measure our ability to fulfil short-term
commitments, we use two ratios:

- Working capital ratio (or current ratio)
- Liquidity test (or quick ratio or acid test ratio).

In both instances, how high the ratio must be depends on
a number of factors in the business, but quite clearly the
current ratio should be higher than 1 to 1 and probably
even higher than 2 to 1. Two means that there are twice
as many current assets as current liabilities.

The formulae for these two ratios are:

$$\text{Working capital ratio} = \frac{\text{Current assets}}{\text{Current liabilities}}$$

$$\text{Liquidity test} = \frac{\text{Current assets} - \text{Stock}}{\text{Current liabilities}}$$

**Note:** When calculating the liquidity or quick ratio you
can also use the following formula as you are calculating
the value of current assets less the value of the stock in
the business. You want to see if you are able to pay your
liabilities with the current assets you have before you need
to sell more stock.

$$\text{Liquidity test} = \frac{\text{Debtors} + \text{Cash}}{\text{Current liabilities}}$$

---

**Practical example**

Extract the following information from the balance sheet for the
2011 financial year:

Current assets (28)      = 845 500
Current liabilities (37)    = 694 080
Stock (29)          = 360 840

---

| | |
|---|---|
| Working capital ratio | $= \dfrac{845\,500}{694\,080}$ |
| | $= 1{,}22{:}1$ |
| Liquidity test | $= \dfrac{845\,500 - 360\,840}{694\,080}$ |
| | $= 0{,}7{:}1$ |

The result of the working capital ratio of R1,22 to R1 means that for every R1 we owe in liabilities, we have current assets to the value of R1,22 to cover the debt. Generally we would like this ratio to work out to R2:R1, meaning that we then have twice as many current assets as current liabilities. If this ratio is too high it may signify that the business has too many current assets or under-uses short-term credit facilities.

The liquidity test or quick ratio measures the business's ability to meet its short-term obligations using its most liquid assets. The result of the liquidity test in our example shows that for every R1 we owe in liabilities, we have current assets worth R0,70 to cover the debt before we have to sell the stock. We are assuming, though, that all our debtors pay us on time and do not default on their payments. It is dangerous to allow these ratios to fall below the 1:1 mark as the business could suffer cash flow problems. Although it looks as though we can cover our debt from the working capital ratio, as soon as we take stock out of the equation, the ratio falls below 1:1. We are now in the position where we will have to increase sales and reduce our stockholding if we have to pay some of our liabilities. The empiric standard for this ratio is R1:R1 and indicates financial health.

Although we must ensure that we have sufficient liquid resources to manage the business, we also do not want too much liquidity. Generally, money that is invested in a liquid form earns us less interest than money that is not. If the working capital ratio is very high it could mean that the business is not using its resources efficiently. If the ratios are low, then you must review the balance of the debtors book, how quickly you are collecting the money owed to the business and also keep a close eye on your stockholding. If your stock value is high but there is a valid reason, such as that more stock was purchased due to an upcoming promotion that will probably be sold off quickly in the near future, then you may be satisfied with a high stock value in the short term. If you purchased extra stock that you did not really need because the supplier was offering it at a reduced price, you run the risk of not being able to sell it and being left with useless or redundant stock.

**Remember:** Money tied up in stock cannot be used more effectively elsewhere. High stockholdings also means increased exposure to risk such as theft, natural disasters, fire, etc. Check the liquidity of the business on a monthly basis.

## Circulation of funds

Capital can only make money when it is kept moving, that is, it passes through the business in its various forms and returns from the customer to complete the cycle. We call this *circulation of funds*. The formula for calculating circulation of funds is:

$$\text{Circulation of funds} = \frac{\text{Annual sales (turnover)}}{\text{Total equity (capital and reserves)}}$$

**Note:** Because we are reviewing the financial statements for a six-month period, the annual sales figure we use will be for this period only.

---

**Practical example**

Extract the following information from the income statement and balance sheet for the 2010 and 2011 periods:

|                      | 2010      | 2011      |
|----------------------|-----------|-----------|
| Annual sales (1)     | 1 538 710 | 1 745 400 |
| Total equity (35)    | 768 070   | 795 860   |
| (Capital and reserves) |         |           |

$$\text{Circulation of funds} = \frac{1\ 538\ 710}{768\ 070} \quad \frac{1\ 745\ 400}{795\ 860}$$

$$= \quad 2 \text{ times} \quad 2{,}2 \text{ times}$$

The total equity figures used in these calculations include the owner's contribution to the business and profits retained from the previous year (reserves). You must decide if you are going to include the retained profits figure as part of this calculation or if you are only going to use the owner's equity. If you use both then you must show the owner's equity (contribution) and retained profits (reserves) separately.

---

This calculation shows us that the money invested in the business circulates through the business twice during the six-month period. If the business operated in much the same way for the rest of the financial year, then it may be safe to assume that the circulation would double to four times per year. The objective here is to use less money (capital) to run the business. It will then circulate through the business more often and therefore make more money or improve the return on equity or investment, as seen in the next section.

## Return on investment

If you decide you want to start a business with money you have saved, you will want to grow or increase your investment in the business. If you are not sure that the business concept will be profitable and that your money will grow, it may be preferable to invest the funds in a bank deposit account or in the stock market where it will at least grow by the current interest rate. The main objective of management is to generate a maximum return on shareholders' investments. Calculating this ratio is probably the best measure of a business's success.

We want to know what return we are getting on the capital we have invested in the business. The calculation is known as the return on equity or return on investment.

$$\text{Return on investment} = \frac{\text{Net profit (before tax)}}{\text{Capital and reserves}} \times 100$$

---

**Practical example**

Extract the following information from the income statement and balance sheet for the 2010 and 2011 periods:

|  | 2010 | 2011 |
|---|---|---|
| Net profit (before tax) (20) | 125 620 | 147 086 |
| Capital and reserves (35) | 768 070 | 795 860 |
| Return on investment | $= \frac{125\ 620}{768\ 070} \times 100$ | $\frac{147\ 086}{795\ 860} \times 100$ |
|  | $= 16{,}36\%$ | $18{,}48\%$ |

Once again, the capital and reserves used in these calculations included the owner's contribution to the business and profits retained from the previous year. You can also use the combined figure, but remember that the retained or undistributed net profit was not originally invested by the owners and has been accumulating.

---

Before we calculated the return on investment, we looked at the number of times the money invested in the business moved through the business during the course of a six-

*Capital can only make money if it is kept moving*

month period. We calculated the circulation of funds to be approximately 2,2. We can use this information and the net profit from the income statement to calculate the return on investment in another way. The net profit margin we worked out earlier for the 2011 period is 8,43%.

Return on investment = Net profit margin (8,43%) × Circulation (2,2)
= 18,55%

If we look at the calculation we see that both the net profit and the circulation of funds impact on the level of return we get on the money we invested in the business. If we had used less capital and increased the circulation of funds to, say, three times, then our return would have been 25,29%. Likewise, if we had increased turnover and/or controlled our cost of sales and expenses more effectively, then we would show a higher net profit, which in turn would have ensured a greater return on investment.

The return on investment figure can now be used to compare the return offered by one business against other investment opportunities as well as other similar businesses (industry benchmarks). As shown in this and in the previous calculations, total assets are sometimes used for capital employed. Complications can arise when long-term funding – loan capital – is provided by someone besides the owners, such as an interest-bearing loan from a bank. If you decide to include loan capital in the capital employed figure, then you may need to add back the interest paid on the loan to the net profit, since this is also part of the return on the capital employed.

## Stock turnover rate

Stock turnover means the number of times in a period that the average stock is used up and replaced. Stock is the most liquid form of the current assets of a business after cash and the debtors. It is for this reason that stock must be closely monitored and controlled. We should also determine what the business's ideal stock turnover rate should be and then

*Return on investment*

periodically calculate the actual stock turnover rate to ensure it is the same as our desired stock turnover rate. Cost of sales is, in effect, sales at cost value. Divide this figure by average stock to determine the stock turnover rate.

**Remember:** This calculation applies to businesses that retail or manufacture products and therefore keep stock in either its final form or raw materials that will be converted to a finished product.

The formula for calculating the stock turnover rate is:

$$\text{Stock turnover rate} = \frac{\text{Cost of sales or goods}}{\text{Average stock at cost price}}$$

**Note:** In order to calculate the average stock you must add together the opening stock and closing stock figures for the period and divide by two.

---

**Practical example**

Extract the following information from the income statement for the 2010 and 2011 financial years:

|  |  | 2010 | 2011 |
|---|---|---|---|
| Cost of sales (2) |  | 1 015 340 | 1 126 420 |
| Opening stock (3) |  | 312 390 | 338 370 |
| Closing stock (5) |  | 338 370 | 360 840 |
| Average stock | $=$ | $\frac{312\,390 + 338\,370}{2}$ | $\frac{338\,370 + 360\,840}{2}$ |
|  | $=$ | 325 380 | 349 605 |
| Stock turnover rate | $=$ | $\frac{1\,015\,340}{325\,380}$ | $\frac{1\,126\,420}{349\,605}$ |
|  | $=$ | 3,12 | 3,22 |

---

Once you have performed the calculation you can then work out the average number of months or days for which stock is held. Remember that the financial statements we have used are for a six-month period and we therefore use six months (half a year) or 182,5 (for days).

| | | | |
|---|---|---|---|
| Average no. of months | $=$ | $\dfrac{6}{3,12}$ | $\dfrac{6}{3,22}$ |
| | $=$ | 1,92 months | 1,86 months |
| Average no. of days | $=$ | $\dfrac{182,5}{3,12}$ | $\dfrac{182,5}{3,22}$ |
| | $=$ | 58 days | 56 days |

The more times we turn over our stock, the more money we make. Therefore, a low stock turnover rate may result in a large portion of our working capital being tied up in stock. Industry dependent of course, it generally holds true that a lower stock turnover means lower profits. It also means higher stockholdings, which presents its own problems, as discussed earlier. A higher stock turnover rate may result in lost sales due to insufficient stock. It is therefore important to have a level of stock relative to sales and adequate to meet customer demand. Stock turnover and the number of days' cover you have in the business must be calculated every month.

## Debtors trading cycle

Debtors are people who owe us money as a result of buying our goods on credit. The debtors trading cycle tells us how long on average it takes debtors to pay us back for the goods they purchased. It shows the effectiveness of credit control in the business.

The information required to calculate this figure includes the value of outstanding debtors from the balance sheet or the debtors journal, as well as the sales or turnover figures of the business from the income statement. Remember that the sales figure on the income statement may include both cash and sales on credit. When calculating the debtors trading cycle you must extract only the credit sales. You should know what portion of total sales is made up of credit sales as you also want to achieve a balance between cash and credit income. In our example, however, we will assume that all sales were made on credit.

Before we can calculate the length of time it takes for our debtors to pay us, we must first calculate the debtor turnover rate.

$$\text{Debtor turnover rate} = \frac{\text{Sales}}{\text{Average debtors}}$$

**Note:** In order to calculate the average debtors, add the opening debtors to the closing debtors for the period and divide by two. If the business has been operational for several years, it is better to take the debtors value for each month, add them all together and divide by 12 to get an average for the year. For the purpose of this example we have used the debtors figure as it is shown on the balance sheet.

$$\text{Debtors trading cycle} = \frac{365}{\text{Debtor turnover rate}}$$

**Practical example**

Extract the following information from the income statement and balance sheet for the 2010 and 2011 financial years:

|  | 2010 | 2011 |
|---|---|---|
| Sales (1) | 1 538 710 | 1 745 400 |
| Average debtors (30) | 490 770 | 445 320 |
| Debtor turnover rate = | $\frac{1\,538\,710}{490\,770}$ | $\frac{1\,745\,400}{445\,320}$ |
| = | 3,13 | 3,92 |

Once you have performed the above calculation you can then work out the average number of months or days it takes for your debtors to pay you.

| Average no. of months | = | 6 | 6 |
|---|---|---|---|
| | | 3,13 | 3,92 |
| | = | 1,92 months | 1,53 months |
| Average no. of days | = | 182,5 | 182,5 |
| | | 3,13 | 3,92 |
| | = | 58 days | 46 days |

The calculations show that we replaced our debtors on average three times during the 2010 financial year and

*Don't carry your debtors for too long*

almost four times in the 2011 year. We can also see from the example that it took our debtors close to two months in 2010 and then only about a month and a half in 2011 on average to pay us. This means that we are selling goods for which we may already have paid and are only recovering our money 45 days to two months after we sold them.

It is important to manage the debtors book efficiently and to ensure that all outstanding debts are followed up on and money collected regularly. One piece of advice I can give you is that when you approve a credit application from a customer you should set realistic credit limits and be very specific regarding your payment terms. When the client reaches that credit limit, no further purchases should be allowed until such time as the money due or a portion of it has been paid. At the end of every month you should print statements and send these to your customers with copies of the relevant invoices attached. Statements should show a breakdown of the customer's account detailing the amount of money due for each trading period. This is known as an *age analysis,* and when a customer owes you money from six months ago, the amount for that period will show under the 180 days column on the age analysis statement. You must try to keep your debtors trading cycle to a minimum – preferably 30 days. This figure will vary from industry to industry. For example, a clothing retailer that allows its customers up to six months to pay will have a longer debtors trading cycle. A long average collection period could indicate that one or more of the following weaknesses exist in the business:

- You are providing credit facilities to customers who are not creditworthy or who have a poor credit history.

- Your billing procedures are slow and you send out invoices and statements late.

- You do not have adequate follow-up procedures in place for slow-paying or defaulting customers.

## Creditors trading cycle

Creditors are businesses or people to whom we owe money as a result of buying their goods on credit instead of paying cash on delivery. The creditors trading cycle tells us how long on average it takes us to pay the creditors for the goods we purchased. Creditors generally arise through stock purchases. If you do not adhere to the suppliers' payment terms and it takes you several months to pay your suppliers, you may land up in a situation where they do not want to supply you anymore or they start charging you interest on overdue accounts.

The figures we need to calculate the creditors trading cycle are purchases from the income and expenses statement or the purchases/creditors journal and average creditors from the balance sheet. Before we can calculate the length of time (in days or months) it takes us to pay our creditors, we must first calculate the creditor turnover rate.

$$\text{Creditor turnover rate} = \frac{\text{Purchases}}{\text{Average creditors}}$$

**Note:** In order to calculate the average creditors, add the opening creditors to the closing creditors for the period and divide by two. If the business has been operational for several years it is better to take the creditors value for each month, add them all together and divide by 12 to get an average for the year. For the purpose of this example we have used the creditors figure as shown on the balance sheet.

$$\text{Creditors trading cycle} = \frac{365}{\text{Creditor turnover rate}}$$

---

**Practical example**

Extract the following information from the income statement and balance sheet for the 2010 and 2011 financial years:

|  | 2010 | 2011 |
|---|---|---|
| Purchases (4) | 1 041 320 | 1 148 890 |
| Average creditors (38) | 618 950 | 685 720 |
| Creditor turnover rate $= \dfrac{1\,041\,320}{618\,950}$ | $\dfrac{1\,148\,890}{685\,720}$ | |
| $=$ 1,68 | 1,68 | |

This means that creditors are paid and replaced by new creditors 1,68 times during each period. Once you have performed this calculation, you can then work out the average number of months or days it takes you to pay your creditors.

| Average no. of months | $= \dfrac{6}{1,68}$ | $\dfrac{6}{1,68}$ |
|---|---|---|
|  | $=$ 3,57 months | 3,57 months |
| Average no. of days | $= \dfrac{182,5}{1,68}$ | $\dfrac{182,5}{1,68}$ |
|  | $=$ 108 days | 108 days |

---

The above calculations show that we paid and replaced our creditors 1,68 times during both periods. In other words, the creditor turnover rate did not change from 2010 to 2011. Because the creditor turnover rate remained the same, we averaged three and a half months to pay our creditors. If we go back and look at the debtors trading cycle for the first year, you will see that it took almost two months for our debtors to pay us, whereas in 2011 it took our debtors only one and a half months to pay their debts. Calculate the creditors trading cycle and payment period every month so that you are aware of how long it is taking you to settle your debt.

In order to ensure good relationships with your suppliers you should adhere to their payment terms and pay your bills on time. You also want to avoid having to pay interest on overdue accounts or having your suppliers cancel your credit facilities as you then have to pay cash for all stock you order at the time of delivery or even source new suppliers. Ideally you want to try to arrange longer payment terms with your suppliers so that you may pay them after you have been paid by the debtors, but in order to do this you must ensure that your debtors pay you on time.

## Interest coverage ratio

Many people starting out in business do not have all the capital necessary to set up the business, fit it out and buy the initial stock. They then approach a financial lending institution such as a bank, or they find a partner who has some capital to invest. This loan capital attracts interest, which must be paid to the lender along with the repayment of the actual loan amount. This is also known as gearing the business. You must ensure that the business will perform sufficiently and make sufficient net profit to cover the loan and interest payments. You must also ensure that if interest rates suddenly increase, the business will still be generating sufficient profit to cover the increase in the interest payments and all creditors.

$$\text{Interest coverage ratio} = \frac{\text{Net profit (before tax and interest)}}{\text{Interest paid}}$$

**Note:** If you look at the income statement you will see that interest is listed as an operational expense and therefore the net profit shown excludes this interest. We must therefore add interest back onto net profit before calculating the interest coverage ratio.

---

**Practical example**

Extract the following information from the income statement for 2011:

Net profit (20) $\quad = \quad$ 147 086

Interest (17) $\quad = \quad$ 24 800

Net profit before interest $\quad = \quad$ 147 086 + 24 800

$\quad = \quad$ 171 886

Interest coverage ratio $\quad = \quad \dfrac{171\ 886}{24\ 800}$

$\quad = \quad$ 6,93:1

---

Net profit before tax and interest equals your free cash flow. The interest coverage ratio reflects the number of times the interest expense is covered by earnings or cash flow. The ratio reveals the magnitude of decline in income that a business can tolerate and still be able to meet its interest payments. Ideally you want the ratio to be 3:1, which means that the business is generating three times as much profit as the interest expense. Perform this calculation every month so that if you see a decline in the ratio you can investigate immediately and take the necessary steps to increase the ratio.

# APPENDIX 1: EXTRACT FROM THE COMPANIES ACT

*The Companies Act 2008 imposes on the directors of a company a duty to make out annual financial statements and to lay them before the annual general meeting.*

1. The directors of a company shall in respect of every financial year of the company cause to be made out in one of the official languages of the Republic annual financial statements and shall lay them before the annual general meeting of the company required to be held in terms of section 179 in respect of that financial year.

2. The annual financial statements required to be made out shall consist of –

   a) a balance sheet, including any notes thereon or document annexed thereto providing information required by this Act;

   b) an income statement, including any similar financial statement where such form is appropriate and including any notes thereon or document annexed there to providing information required by this Act;

   c) a cash flow statement;

   d) a directors' report complying with the requirements of this Act; and

   e) an auditor's report (only if the company is required to be audited).

3. The annual financial statements of a company shall, in conformity with generally accepted accounting practice, fairly present the state of affairs of the company and its business as at the end of the financial year concerned and the profit or loss of the company for that financial

year and shall for that purpose be in accordance with and include at least the matters prescribed by the Act in so far as they are applicable, and comply with any other requirements of this Act.

4.  a) Any director or officer of a company who fails to take all reasonable steps to comply or to secure compliance with the provisions of the relevant sections or with any other requirements of this Act as to matters to be stated in annual financial statements, shall be guilty of an offence.

# APPENDIX 2: FINANCIAL REPORTING REQUIREMENTS AND THE PUBLIC INTEREST SCORE

The Companies Act of 2008 classifies companies as small, medium and large. The classification is important because it simplifies financial reporting requirements for small companies. Seeing that existing CCs fall into the same categories since the new Act took effect, no specific reference will be made to CCs.

Depending on its size, a company may have a choice between preparing its annual financial statements (AFSs) internally or have them prepared independently. However, accepted accounting standards and requirements for either auditing or an independent review must be observed.

In terms of the Act, every company must prepare an AFS but some companies do not need to have it either independently reviewed or audited. The main determining factor is the company's Public Interest Score (PIS), a set of four factors, namely:

a) the number of shareholders

b) the number of employees

c) the rand value of annual sales

d) the rand amount of unsecured outstanding debt.

### *Audit or independent review?*

When does a company need to be audited? If a company holds assets in a fiduciary capacity for persons who are not related to the company and the aggregate value of such assets held at any time during the financial year exceeds R5 million and/or the company's PIS is 350 or more (if the AFS was compiled independently by an independent accounting professional), or 100 or more (if the AFS was compiled internally) then the AFS must be audited.

When does a company need to have its AFS independently reviewed? An independent review of a company's AFS must be carried out if the company has a PIS of at least 100 by an auditor, or less than 100 by a person who is qualified to hold the function of accounting officer in a CC. (Because an independent review is less thorough, and therefore less time consuming, it is usually significantly cheaper than a full audit.)

### *Calculating the Public Interest Score*

The PIS must be calculated at the end of each financial year. This is done as follows:

a) Number of shareholders – 1 point per shareholder.

b) Number of employees – 1 point for each employee, based on the average number of employees employed during the year.

c) Rand value of annual sales – 1 point for every R1 million (or part thereof) of annual sales.

d) Rand amount of unsecured outstanding debt – 1 point for every R1 million (or part thereof) of unsecured loans outstanding at financial year-end.

# APPENDIX 3: TAX RELIEF FOR SMALL BUSINESSES

*Tax relief for Small Business Corporations (SBCs)*

*The following is an extract from SARS's Small Business Guide relating to tax relief for small businesses.*

The small business corporation regime allows three major concessions to companies and CCs which comply with the following requirements:

- The shareholders or members must be natural persons (individuals) and must hold interest of the company/CC.

- Shareholders or members may not hold any shares or interest in the equity of any other company (excluding shares in listed companies, a participatory interest in a collective investment scheme or an interest in a company as contemplated in section 10(1)(e)(i); (ii) or (iii) of the Income Tax Act (body corporates)).

- The gross income of the corporation for the tax year may not exceed R14 million.

- Not more than 20% of the total of all receipts and accruals (other than those of a capital nature) and all capital gains of the company/CC may consist collectively of investment income and income from rendering a personal service. Investment income includes interest, dividends, royalties, rental and annuities. Personal services are services in the field of, for example, accounting, real estate and engineering which are performed personally by a person holding an interest in the company/CC.

- The company/CC may not be an employment company (i.e. a labour broker without an exemption certificate or a personal service company).

The *first concession* is to be taxed on the basis of a split rate system, i.e. SBCs pay no tax at all on income up to R57 000 per annum then tax at a rate of 10% on taxable income between R57 001 and R300 000. Thereafter tax is payable at a rate of 30% for every R1 in excess of R150 000.

The *second concession* is the immediate write-off of all plant and machinery used in a process of manufacturing in the tax year it is brought into use.

The *third concession* is the double deduction of any expenditure and losses actually incurred by the SBC in the tax year it commences trading. However, this double deduction is capped, with the figure possibly changing from one tax year to the next. Assuming that the double deduction is capped at R20 000, if the SBC incurs R100 000 deductible expenditure in the tax year during which it commences with its trading activities, it will receive a total deduction of R120 000.

For further details refer to the SARS website (www.sars.gov.za).

### Tax relief for very small businesses

Very small businesses – those with annual sales below R1 million – may be able to benefit by registering for turnover tax. Turnover tax registration is open to companies and existing CCs. It is a substitute for income tax, capital gains tax and secondary tax on companies. The business is also exempt from having to register for VAT because the threshold for compulsory registration is R1 million.

Turnover tax simplifies the accounting and record keeping process because it is based on sales and calculated with the help of a rates table. For example, at the time of going to print, the tax payable on a turnover of between R500 001 and R750 000 is R8 000 plus 5% of the amount above R500 001. Rates change – consult www.sars.gov.za for current rates.

Depending on the type of business, this simplified system of taxation may come at a high price. Businesses registered for turnover tax will not be able to apply for voluntary registration for VAT purposes. It follows that they will be unable to claim back input tax for purchases made. This puts them at an immediate disadvantage vis-à-vis their competitors who are registered for VAT and therefore entitled to reclaim input tax.

# APPENDIX 4: TABLE OF FINANCIAL BENCHMARKS PER INDUSTRY

Margins, expenses and profitability vary for different industries and sectors. It is important that you find out what the norms and benchmarks are for your industry. We have provided you with some guidelines for several industries. Please note that these guidelines are purely an indication of what you may expect to achieve in different businesses and to assist you in determining where your business should be on average. Remember that business outcomes may differ substantially from one region to another. Speak to other business people in the same industry and area and enquire as to what margins and returns they achieve in their own businesses.

The industry average benchmarks were obtained from Marican Registered Accountants & Auditors, Johannesburg, and are based on financial results achieved by its clients across these industries.

***Comments***

- In manufacturing, staff costs and rental expenses are generally taken into account when the cost of sales is calculated. The staff costs and rental percentages provided on the following page are for additional staff (not manufacturing) such as administrative and marketing staff and for other office or warehouse space, which is why these averages are so low.

- When calculating cost of sales in a restaurant versus a fast-food outlet, the only expense item that must be included is the cost of packaging. Generally, a take-out outlet would have relatively high packaging costs in relation to turnover, whereas a restaurant would spend far less.

| Measurement | Manufacturing | Service | Restaurants | Fast food | Retail food | Retail clothing & others | Consulting | Software development | Hospitality |
|---|---|---|---|---|---|---|---|---|---|
| Gross profit % | 25–30% | 40–45% | 60% | 55–60% | 50% | 80% | 90% | 80–90% | 40% |
| Staff costs | 8% | 16–18% | 15% | 15% | 18% | 18% | 45% | 10% | 20% |
| Rental | 1% | 5–10% | 10% | 10% | 10% | 10% | 5–10% | 5–10% | 5% |
| Fixed costs | 10% | 25% | 5–8% | 10% | 5–8% | 5–8% | 10% | 20% | 5% |
| Net profit % | 5–8% | 15–18% | 10–15% | 15–20% | 10–15% | 15–20% | 25% | 40% | 5–10% |

- Margins are very low in retail food operations such as supermarkets as these businesses rely on volume trade, whereas retail clothing, furniture, décor, stationery, etc. attract a higher mark-up and therefore produce a better gross margin.

- Consultancies generally sell a service (or intellectual property) as opposed to a physical profit and will generally have a very high gross profit. You may find in consulting that staff costs are factored in as a cost of sales, in which case the gross margin may be smaller, but then the staff costs would be lower. Consulting firms produce a very high net profit margin when compared to other industries.

- Software development attracts high initial development costs as human resources and time are used to develop the product, so at the outset the gross profit may be smaller. Once the product has been developed, all that is required are ongoing upgrades, which are far less time and labour intensive, and the profitability of the product therefore increases. This type of business produces a fairly high net profit when compared to other industries. Depending on future product development plans, the business owner could see an increase in the net profit in the long term.

- However, the business will always require administration, marketing and product support staff and therefore attracts the costs associated with this expense.

- The hospitality industry is very broad as an operation can range from a hotel with 100 bedrooms, a restaurant and bar as well as conference facilities to a small three-bedroom bed and breakfast. Each area of a hotel will have its own profit centre that attracts different margins. For example, the bar may have a gross margin of up to

60% or 70% whereas the rooms division may be as low as 20% because it is far more labour intensive and must also be cleaned daily. Also to be considered is whether the hotel (property) is being financed by a bank, or whether the bed and breakfast property is owned by the owners of the business and used for business purposes, as this will impact on rental payments for the premises so the rental percentage could vary substantially.

# APPENDIX 5: GLOSSARY OF FINANCIAL TERMS

**Assets, fixed and current:** Fixed assets form part of the business infrastructure, e.g. land, buildings, vehicles and equipment. Current assets are assets directly related to the business's main trading activity, e.g. cash, stock, raw materials, work in progress and debtors.

**Balance sheet:** Provides a summary of the business at a specific point in time and shows where the money in the business has come from (owner's/shareholders' investment, loan capital or reserves) as well as where the money is being used (assets, working capital or investments).

**Benchmark:** (company or industry standard or industry norm) Setting standardised figures in the form of a percentage to monitor business expenses from one period to the next so that we can compare them from one period to another and to industry averages.

**Breakeven:** (breakeven analysis or breakeven point) Reflects the amount of sales or income required to ensure sufficient gross profit to pay all business operating expenses where the business makes a zero net profit, i.e. neither a profit nor a loss.

**Capital:** (equity, funds, investments or shareholder's equity) Money that the owners or shareholders invest in the business generally in exchange for part-ownership of the business and a share in future profits.

**Capital expenditure:** (capex) Spending money on fixed assets such as land, buildings or vehicles that are required for the business to generate sales/income.

**Cash flow:** The amount of money that flows into and out of the business during a specific period.

**Cost of sales:** (cost of goods sold) The total costs incurred in getting a finished product to the customer. In manufacturing, it is the total cost of making the product and can include raw material costs, transport, storage, labour costs, etc. In retail, it is generally the purchase price of stock and may include transport costs, import duties, etc.

**Creditors:** (accounts payable) Companies or individuals such as suppliers who have supplied the business with goods or services and where payment is made on a future date. The creditors list or age analysis shows the amounts due to creditors and when these payments are due.

**Creditors trading cycle:** (creditors period) The average length of time it takes the business to pay its short-term debts.

**Debtors:** (accounts receivable) A customer who owes the business money for purchases made on credit. The debtors age analysis is a summary of the amounts that debtors owe as well as for how long the debt has been outstanding.

**Debtors trading cycle:** (debtors period, debtors outstanding ratio) The average length of time it takes debtors to pay their accounts.

**Expenses:** (operating costs/expenses or overheads) Costs incurred in the operation of the business that are not directly related to the product, e.g. rental, salaries and wages, utilities and administration costs. Can also be split as fixed costs and variable costs. Fixed costs are expenses that generally do not change in the short term such as long-term leases. Variable costs are expenses that fluctuate such as telephone, contract labour, etc.

**Financial period:** (accounting period or financial year) This is usually 12 months but can be shorter or longer during the first year of operation.

**Gross profit (GP):** The amount of money left after the cost of sales has been deducted from the sales.

**Gross profit percentage:** (gross profit margin) The actual gross profit calculated as a percentage of the sales.

**Income statement:** (income and expense statement, or profit and loss statement or account) The financial statement that summarises the sales, expenses and profitability of the business over a period such as a week, month, year, etc.

**Liabilities:** Money owed by the business and that can be categorised as long-term liabilities such as loan repayments, and short-term liabilities which include bank overdrafts, money owed to creditors, etc.

**Liquidity:** (solvency) A measurement of the business's capability to manage its current assets and have sufficient working capital to pay its short-term liabilities.

**Loan capital:** (loan finance or long-term loan) Finance obtained for the business by borrowing funds. The lenders do not have any ownership in the business and expect to be paid back either in a lump sum or in instalments over a period of time. Loan capital generally attracts interest and both the loan and interest must be repaid regardless of whether or not the business is profitable.

**Net profit:** The amount of money left after all expenses have been deducted from the gross profit. State whether this figure is inclusive or exclusive of tax. Net profit is shown as net profit before/after tax.

**Net profit percentage:** (net profit margin) The actual net profit calculated as a percentage of sales or turnover.

**Ratios:** (performance ratios or productivity ratios) Used to make comparisons between two figures.

**Reserves:** (retained profit) Money that has been retained in the business from previous periods' profits and carried forward into the next period for use in the future.

**Return on equity:** (return on investment or return on capital employed) The value of return an investor can expect for lending the business a certain amount of money. The return can be in the form of dividends paid annually out of profits or from the sale of shares after a period of time at a higher value than the purchase value.

**Safety margin:** Shows the amount of sales that can be lost before the business begins trading below the breakeven point and therefore begins trading at a loss.

**Sales:** (income, turnover or revenue. Fee income is used in professional practices or consultancies.) The income generated in the business during the normal course of its trading activities.

**Stock:** (inventory) The total of all raw materials, value of work in progress and completed goods that are sold to customers.

**Stock turnover rate:** (stock turn, stock days or stock turnaround ratio) The number of times in a period that the average stock is used up and replaced. Calculate how long stock will last by dividing the number of days in the period by the stock turnover rate.

**Working capital:** This is the amount of money required to finance ongoing operations until such time as the business's cash flow can take care of ongoing expenses.

# APPENDIX 6: CALCULATIONS OVERVIEW

| Calculation | Why do it? | Using the results |
|---|---|---|
| Cost of sales = Opening stock + Purchases − Closing stock | To calculate what it costs the business to get the finished product to the customer | Ensures performance is in line with budgets and industry norms; monitors cost effectiveness/ profitability of producing the product; monitors and reduces wastage, shrinkage |
| Gross profit = Sales − Cost of sales | To determine the amount of money left to pay expenses after cost of sales has been deducted; provides an indication of the effectiveness of pricing policy and purchase and production controls | Ensures performance is in line with budgets and industry norms; assists with management and control of stock; provides an indication of whether sales (or selling prices) are correct; monitors cost effectiveness/ profitability of producing the product |
| Gross profit margin = $\frac{\text{Gross profit}}{\text{Sales}} \times 100$ | To avoid comparing isolated figures, which can be misleading | Compares results to previous periods and budgets; manages operational performance more effectively |

*Finance in your own business*

| Calculation | Why do it? | Using the results |
|---|---|---|
| Breakeven point = $\frac{\text{Expenses}}{\text{Gross profit margin}}$ | To have a clear understanding of what sales the business must achieve to cover the cost of sales and pay operating expenses | Know the breakeven so that sales can be monitored throughout the period as this will indicate when the business has reached the breakeven point |
| Safety margin = $\frac{\text{Actual sales} - \text{Breakeven sales}}{\text{Actual Sales}} \times 100$ | Indication of the amount of sales that can be lost before the business starts operating at below the breakeven point | This is the safety net in the business and shows the amount of sales the business can lose before it finds itself in a position of not being able to pay the bills; know the safety margin and breakeven point so that corrective action can be taken timeously |
| Average mark-up $= \frac{\text{Gross profit}}{\text{Cost of sales}} \times 100$ | To determine the selling price of a product taking the desired gross profit into account | Assists in ensuring desired gross profits are met; mark-up is calculated to determine the selling price, which should then be reviewed to determine if it is competitive |
| Benchmarking expenses = $\frac{\text{Expense}}{\text{Gross profit}} \times 100$ OR $\frac{\text{Expense}}{\text{Turnover}} \times 100$ | To monitor expenses from one period to the next and ensure these are in line with budgets | Compare actual expenses to budgeted figures and to previous periods to ensure profitability and control |

| Calculation | Why do it? | Using the results |
|---|---|---|
| Staff productivity ratio = $\frac{\text{Turnover}}{\text{Staff costs}}$ | To ensure staff employed in the business are productive, effective and contribute to the growth of the business | Monitor staff productivity to sales, and if sales decrease or are lower than budgeted, reduce staff costs |
| Net profit margin = $\frac{\text{Net profit}}{\text{Turnover}} \times 100$ | To show the actual net profit as a percentage of turnover to be able to compare profitability accurately from one period to the next | The level of profitability shows the effectiveness of operations controls: the higher the net profit, the higher the sales and the better controlled stock and expenses were; if profits or margins are low (or not in line with what was budgeted), then all areas of the operation must be reviewed and controls put in place to ensure future goals are met |
| Net profit ratio = $\frac{\text{Turnover}}{\text{Net profit}}$ | To show the amount of net profit made per R1 of turnover | Interest, tax and dividends are paid out of net profit (after cost of sales and operational costs) |

*Finance in your own business*

| Calculation | Why do it? | Using the results |
|---|---|---|
| Working capital = Current assets − Current liabilities | To know how much surplus liquid funds are available in the business | Working capital is the amount of money left over after all current liabilities have been paid; owners/managers must know how much funds are available to be able to make decisions regarding stock purchases, operational expenses and purchasing new equipment, and to plan ahead for unexpected occurrences |
| Working capital ratio (current ratio) $= \dfrac{\text{Current assets}}{\text{Current liabilities}}$ | To ensure the business's ability to meet its financial obligations | Ensure that the ratio averages 2:1 and take quick action if the ratio falls below this mark; monitor the amount of money tied up in stock and ensure that stock moves through the business at the desired rate |
| Liquidity test (acid test, quick ratio) $= \dfrac{\text{Current assets} - \text{Stock}}{\text{Current liabilities}}$ | To ensure the business's ability to meet its financial obligations | Ensure that the ratio averages 1:1 and take quick action if the ratio falls below this mark; monitor the amount of money tied up |

| Calculation | Why do it? | Using the results |
|---|---|---|
| | | in stock and ensure that stock moves through the business at the desired rate |
| Circulation of funds = $$\frac{\text{Annual sales (turnover)}}{\text{Total equity (capital \& reserves)}}$$ | To determine the rate at which the funds used in the business pass through the business during a specific period | Money invested in the business makes more money when it is kept moving through the business; aim to use less money, thus allowing it to move through the business more often and improve the return on investment; if the circulation is slow or slows down during a period, invest some of the equity elsewhere for a better return, and reduce funds so that they circulate through the business more often |
| Return on investment = $$\frac{\text{Net profit (before tax)}}{\text{Capital \& reserves}} \times 100$$ | To monitor the growth and value of the investment in the business | Monitor the return on investment to ensure that investors are seeing an adequate return on their money; if the return is lower than expected, review the |

| Calculation | Why do it? | Using the results |
|---|---|---|
| | | profitability of the operation and, if possible, invest some of the equity where a better return can be guaranteed |
| Stock turnover rate = $\dfrac{\text{Cost of sales/goods}}{\text{Average stock at cost price}}$ | To ensure that stock moves through the business at the desired rate; to minimise shrinkage and defunct, spoilt stock | Minimise funds being tied up in stock for long periods; use and replace stock regularly to ensure a minimum number of days stock coverage; ensure that sufficient stock is kept to meet customer demand |
| Debtor turnover rate = $\dfrac{\text{Sales}}{\text{Average debtors}}$  Debtors trading cycle = $\dfrac{365}{\text{Debtor turnover rate}}$ | To know the value of what debtors owe the business as well as how long it takes debtors to pay | Know the portion of credit versus cash sales and manage the outstanding debt effectively to ensure that debtors pay on the due date; implement effective follow-up processes for defaulting debtors |

| Calculation | Why do it? | Using the results |
|---|---|---|
| Creditor turnover rate = $\dfrac{\text{Purchases}}{\text{Average creditors}}$<br><br>Creditors trading cycle = $\dfrac{365}{\text{Creditor turnover rate}}$ | To know the value of what is owed to suppliers and other creditors as well as how long the business takes to pay the supplier | Maintain good relationships with suppliers and creditors by ensuring that their payment periods are honoured; this will also minimise interest being charged on overdue accounts; manage the payment period so that creditors are paid within the same time period as the debtors, as this promotes a positive cash flow |
| Interest coverage ratio = $\dfrac{\text{Net profit (before tax \& interest)}}{\text{Interest paid}}$ | To ensure the business makes sufficient net profit to repay the actual loan amount as well as the interest that the loan attracts | Know the number of times the interest expense is covered by earnings or net profits so that loan repayments can be met or corrective action taken timeously; check turnover and performance and ensure that all expense budgets are being met |

# INDEX

## A

accounting 10, 13, 57-8, 148, 172
  periods 77-8, 86
  records 13,15
  software 97,111
acid test ratio 45, 90, 152
administration 8, 9, 76, 177
administrator 17
advertising 69, 76, 99, 123, 126, 148
age analysis 163
agreement *see* written agreement
annual financial statements (AFSs) 79, 168, 170-1
  plan 108
annuities 172
asset(s) 38, 74, 79, 84, 107, 179
  current, 44-5, 81-3, 90, 93, 121, 127, 149-53, 158, 179
  fixed, 61, 77, 81-2, 86, 95, 101, 121, 127, 179
  liquid, 85, 90
  management 101
  quick, 91
  value, 29
asset finance *see* finance
audit 170-1
audited accounts 81

## B

balance sheet 13, 15, 43, 60, 79-81, 83, 85-90, 118, 124-5, 127, 142, 149, 151, 155, 160-1, 164-5, 168, 179
bank
  accounts 67
  balance 97-9
  charges 98, 105, 148
  commercial, 14, 21, 38
  finance *see* finance
  loan 36, 95
  overdraft 21-2, 24, 26, 82-4, 91, 93, 102, 104, 148, 151
  statement 67-8, 73
benchmarking 44, 114, 138, 184
benchmarks 39, 129, 131, 142, 158, 175, 179
blueprint for business success 34
bond 16, 32, 37
borrowing 14, 83-4, 94, 96
brand name 33, 41
branding 55-6
breakeven analysis 44
  point 42, 44, 116, 119, 133-6, 179, 184
  bridging finance *see* finance
budget 54, 62-3, 106-7, 109-116, 119, 129, 131-2, 138, 142, 148
  facilities 23
business accounting 10
  administration 8, 9
  calculations 118-9, 124, 128

concepts 41, 156
expenses 44, 50, 63-5, 67-70, 72-6, 87, 95, 119, 129, 138
failure 119, 142, 166, 180
finance *see* finance
income 66-8
management 6, 20
objective 41
partners 19, 20, 48
performance 14, 90, 118
transactions 63

## C

capital *see also* loan capital, working capital 27, 30-1, 83, 85, 92, 179
  base 17
  expenses (capex) 77, 147, 148-9, 179
  gains tax *see* tax
cash assets 44, 82-5, 93-4
  accounting 67, 90-2
  budgeting 26, 54, 63
  flow 197
  management 100, 102, 104, 106-7, 109, 115, 121, 168
  performance 14, 19, 28, 60, 62, 86, 88-9, 91-6, 101, 103, 149, 153
  profitability 114, 119, 146-7, 167
  projection 43, 45, 49, 54, 97-9, 105, 110, 112, 147-8
calculations

average, 143
average creditors, 164
benchmarking expenses, 138, 184
breakeven point, 42, 44, 133, 135-6, 184
business, 128
circulation of funds, 187
cost of sales, 129-30, 183
creditor turnover rate, 164-5
creditors trading cycle, 164, 189
current ratio, 121
debtor turnover rate, 164, 189
debtors trading cycle, 121, 161-3, 188
expenses, 138
funds, 154
gross-profit, 129-30, 137, 183-4
interest coverage ratio, 166-7, 189
liquidity test, 152-3, 186
margin, 137
mark-up, 136-7, 184
net profit margin, 145-6, 185
net profit ratio, 145-7, 185
operational, 128
Public Interest Score (PIS), 171
quick ratio, 121, 153
ratio, 142
 return on investment, 156-8, 187

calculations
    safety margin, 133-4, 184
    staff productivity ratio, 143-5, 185
    stock turnover rate, 92, 121, 158-60, 188
    working capital ratio, 151-4, 186
circulation of funds 154-5, 157, 187
close corporations (CCs) 57-8, 60-1, 65, 78-9, 170, 172-3
Close Corporations Act of 1984 57-8, 61
closing stock *see also* stock 73-4, 126, 159
community financing *see* finance
Companies Act, Act of 71 of 2008 57-8, 60-1, 168-70
competition 41, 44, 46,49, 68, 89, 108, 122
Consumer Protection Act 32, 34
corporation tax *see* tax
    cost of sales 68-75, 91-2, 121, 123, 126, 129-30, 132, 145, 159, 175, 177, 180
cost(s) 60, 74, 116
    capital, 112
    development, 117
    fixed, 112, 115
    information, 63, 111
    production, 73, 75
    recording 68, 77
    saving 102
    variable, 112

credit 23, 91, 88
    agreement 25
    application 163
    balance 21
    card 23, 37, 73
    control 88, 101, 160
    extended, 55, 95
    facilities 142, 153, 163
    information 37
    limit 23, 37, 163
    policy 100
    rating 26
    risk 23
    sales 45, 104, 161
    terms 88, 95, 100
creditors 79, 84, 88, 91, 121, 127, 147-8, 151, 164-5, 180, 189
    trading cycle 164-5, 180
    average 164
criminal offences 37
current account 24, 84, 93
    assets *see* assets
    liabilities 44-5, 81-3, 85, 87, 90, 149-152
    ratio 44, 90, 121, 152
customer base 12
    demand 142
    management 100
    services 42, 122, 124
customers 5, 6, 39, 92, 95, 82, 84, 88, 94, 104, 108

**D**
debit balance 21
debt 84, 170-1
debtors 23, 44-5, 61, 86, 91, 119, 121, 127, 147-8, 151,

153, 160-3, 166, 180
age analysis 54, 163
outstanding ratio 45
trading cycle 121, 160-2, 163, 165, 180
turnover 91, 161, 163
defensive interval 91
deposit 26, 67-8, 93-4, 100
depreciation 69, 70, 74, 76, 84, 86, 120, 126, 146
discount(s) 89, 100, 119, 123
dividend payout 20, 84, 95
policy 18
dividends 84-5, 87, 105, 126, 145, 146, 172

**E**
efficiency ratio 90-1
employee(s) 17, 61, 72, 75, 103, 124, 170-1
employment 1, 37
entrepreneurs 1, 3, 4, 28, 46
ethics 32
equipment 8, 41, 68, 76-7, 86, 96, 122
equity 12-3, 15-6, 20, 27, 60, 83, 91, 107, 127, 154-6, 172, 179
finance *see* finance
return on, 155, 182
sweat, 28-9
expenditure 64, 87, 100, 112, 115, 138
expenses *see* business expenses

**F**
factoring 23, 95, 100
failure 119-20
finance 3, 4, 6, 12, 15

asset, 25-6
bank 15, 21, 178
bridging, 21
business, 12, 31-2
charges 76
community, 30
equity, 12-3, 15, 21
house 23, 26
loan, 3, 12-5, 21, 27, 38, 61, 84-7, 89, 92, 96, 102, 105
short term, 23-4, 44, 93
soft loan, 27-8
term loan, 24-5
financial accounting 58-61
funding 3, 4, 15, 23, 26, 28, 32, 35, 41, 46-7, 50, 53, 154
information 38, 87
management 9, 46
performance 9, 108
period 77, 125, 142, 280
projections 11, 35, 42-3, 45-6, 48, 53, 55, 115, 119
reporting 9, 170
statements 60, 80, 87, 117-8, 120, 124-8, 132, 154, 160, 168-9, 170-1
year 61, 77, 78, 125, 134, 162, 168
fixed asset *see* asset
forecasting 60, 62-3, 94, 96-9, 104, 106, 108, 110, 112, 114
franchising 33-4
funders 9, 39, 41, 44, 47, 50, 52, 95
funding *see* financial funding

**G**
gearing 89, 91, 166-7
general expenses *see* overheads
Global Entrepreneurship Monitor (GEM) 3
goodwill 12-3, 29, 82
gross profit (GP) 44, 69, 70, 73, 118-9, 126, 129-30, 132-3, 138, 147, 176-7, 181
gross profit margin 130-2, 119, 136-7, 177, 181
growth potential 20, 48-9
guarantee 12, 26, 32

**H**
hire purchase 25, 37, 101, 105

**I**
income 64, 67, 70, 73, 87, 95, 100, 115, 172
statement 38, 43, 60, 64-6, 68-75, 77, 79, 87-8, 113, 118, 124-6, 128, 132, 149, 155, 157, 159, 161, 166-8, 181
tax 92, 95, 173
Income Tax Act 172
income tax returns 61, 65
infrastructure 7, 8, 34, 41
input tax 174
intellectual property rights 82
interest 12, 15, 21, 23-4, 26, 49, 67, 76, 85, 104, 126,166-7, 172, 189
coverage ratio *see*

gearing
payments 14-5, 21, 88, 148, 158, 167
rates 24, 31, 85, 91, 121, 156, 166
inventory 63, 84, 88-9, 182
investment 12-3, 17, 19, 20, 22, 24, 30, 39, 52, 82, 84, 95, 119, 127, 155, 172, 179
investors 12-3, 29, 30, 42, 47-8, 64, 79-81, 95

**L**
labour legislation 17
lease 68, 96, 101, 141, 148
payments 105
lenders 15, 27, 32, 80-1, 91 95
letters of guarantee 26
liability 13, 15, 38, 79, 84, 90, 149, 152-3, 181
loan account 15
agreement 15, 24
capital 15, 24, 158, 166, 181
finance *see* finance
funding 12
proposal 24
schemes 34
repayments 14, 30, 49, 95, 138, 147-9
long term borrowing *see* borrowing
liquid assets *see* assets
liquidity 18, 90, 150, 154, 181
ratio 90
test 152-3, 186
liquidation 12

loss 44, 54, 64-6, 68, 76, 87, 173

**M**
management 123
accounts 9, 58-9, 61-3, 87, 102
decisions 19, 39
margins 114, 175, 177, 137
mark-up 11, 136-7
marketing 42, 47, 69,102, 110, 123, 140-1, 177
manufacturing 41, 173, 175
micro lenders 31-2
mortgage 16, 32, 61, 65
motor vehicle expenses 71, 74, 76-7, 99, 126, 139, 140

**N**
National Credit Act 32
net profit 69, 74, 118, 119, 126, 157-8, 166-7, 176-7, 181
margin 145-6, 157, 177, 181, 185
ratio 145-7

**O**
operating expenses 44, 91, 95, 122, 133-4, 145, 166, 180
income 69, 70, 73
opening stock *see also* stock 73-4, 126, 159
overdraft *see* bank overdraft
overheads 71-2, 75, 111, 122
overtrading 54

ownership 12, 17, 24-6

**P**
patents 82
Pay as You Earn (PAYE) 82, 143
payment controls 89
terms 91, 100, 115
personal assets 16
brand 55-6
details 36-7
petty cash 65, 73
plant 86, 173
presentation 47, 51-2
private company 57, 60, 78-9
profit margins 104, 121, 123,145-6, 185
profits 5, 12-5, 18, 20, 28-9, 44, 60-1, 64-6, 68, 81, 84-5, 87, 92, 94, 116, 120
profitability 6, 90, 119, 121-2, 130
projections *see* financial projections
Public Interest Score (PIS) 170-1

**Q**
quick ratio 45, 90, 121, 152, 153, 186
quick assets *see* assets

**R**
ratio analysis 90, 142
raw materials 8, 74, 84, 95, 102-4, 112, 129, 150, 159
rebate *see* tax rebate
record keeping 63-5
rental 10, 11, 25-6, 67, 95, 126, 141, 148, 172, 175-6, 178

residual value 25-6
repayments 12, 27-8, 38
risks 11, 17, 20, 23, 26

**S**
sales 68, 92, 182
    accounting 59, 62,
    87, 110, 107, 126,
    143-4, 170
    forecasting 2-4,
    111-2
    performance 11, 53-
    4, 69, 114-5, 133
    record 66-7, 72
safety margin 133-4,
    119, 182
salaries 9, 17, 20, 29,
    74-5, 94-5, 97, 105,
    126, 141, 143, 148
savings 15, 95
    account 30-1, 37
secondary tax *see* tax
security 25, 27
self-employed 74, 77
sequestration 37
share capital 85, 105
shares 12, 18-9, 29, 92
shareholders 12-3,
    15-8, 79, 84, 95,
    170-72
    agreement 18
    equity 13, 179
shrinkage 132
    short term loans *see*
    finance
sleeping partners 18-9
small business 1, 3, 5,
    15, 19, 21-2, 27-8,
    32, 70, 109, 172
Small Business
    Corporations
    (SBCs) 172-3
soft loans *see* finance
sole trader 60-1
South African

Revenue Services
    (SARS) 58, 60, 64,
    70, 72, 79-81, 86-7,
    101, 127, 172-3
staff 5, 9, 39, 41, 94,
    102, 111, 122-4,
    141-2, 175
    costs 74, 124, 176-7
    productivity ratio
    123, 124, 143-5, 185
stakeholders 5, 30, 39,
    42, 59, 64, 84, 92,
    156, 170-1
stock 44-5, 75, 89,
    95-6, 102, 119,
    121, 123, 132, 150,
    152, 154, 182
    exchange 20
    level 88-9, 92, 100,
    147
    market 92, 156
    turnover 45, 92,
    121, 123, 158-60,
    182, 188
stokvels 30
supplier management
    100,102
supplies 8, 41
suppliers 5, 6, 8, 9, 25,
    39, 55, 59, 72, 84,
    89, 91-2, 94, 122,
    164, 166
surety 16, 24, 38
sweat equity *see* equity

**T**
target market 11, 41-2
tax(es) 65, 69, 70, 74,
    76, 95, 105
    capital gains, 173
    corporation, 95
    deduction 26, 173
    legislation 78
    liability 64
    rebate 70

rates 70
    relief 172-3
    return 64-5, 80
    payments 65
taxation 101, 174
theft 121, 124, 132
Total Entrepreneurial
    Activity index 3
trade creditors 44, 88
    debtors 88
    unions 80
trademark 33, 82
turnover 66, 115, 121-
    2, 125, 130, 138,
    140-1, 145, 161,
    173, 175, 182
tax 173-4

**U**
Unemployment
    Insurance Fund
    (UIF) 143
utilities 8, 26

**V**
Value-added tax
    (VAT) 71-2, 82,
    92, 95, 101, 130,
    137-8, 148, 173-4
venture capital
    funding 20
venture capitalist
    48-50

**W**
wages 95, 99, 105,
    126, 143, 148
wastage 42
windfall 12, 20
written agreement 18,
    19, 23-4, 28
working capital 23-4,
    34, 84, 111, 114,
    120-1, 147, 149,
    151-2, 160, 182
    ratio 152-4, 186